Fly Tying for Beginners

Geoffrey Bucknall

Fly Tying for Beginners

Illustrated by Keith Linsell *and* Ted Andrews

With a Foreword by Dermot Wilson

Ernest Benn Limited
London & Tonbridge

Other books by Geoffrey Bucknall

Fly-Fishing Tactics on Still Water
Big Pike
Fishing Days
Fly-Fishing Tactics on Rivers
Reservoir Fly Fishing
Book of Fly Fishing

Other books in the
Benn Fishing Handbooks Series

The Super Flies of Still Water
John Goddard

Fifty Favourite Nymphs
T. Donald Overfield

Floatmaker's Manual
Bill Watson

A Manual of Sea Fishing Baits
Hugh Stoker

Published by
Ernest Benn Limited
25 New Street Square, London, EC4A 3JA
& Sovereign Way, Tonbridge, Kent, TN9 1RW

First published 1967
Second edition 1973
Second impression 1974
Third edition 1979
© Geoffrey Bucknall 1967, 1973, 1979

Printed and bound in Great Britain by
Fakenham Press Limited, Fakenham, Norfolk
ISBN 0 510 21110–0
        0 510 21112–7 Paperback

Foreword

by DERMOT WILSON

At this moment Geoffrey Bucknall could perhaps be reflecting that his first million was the hardest to make – his first million flies. But this is highly unlikely, since he has the gift of remembering that the most difficult fly of all for most people is the very first one. The next 999,999 are child's play in comparison with the decision to start tying flies at all.

What is it that holds so many of us back? Personally I am sure that it is neither more nor less than naked fear – fear that we shall never master so intricate and so apparently near-miraculous an art. Our fears may only be fed still further if we happen to overhear one or two of the arch-priests of fly-dressing tongue-wagging about capes and herls and flosses and tippets and tinsels and tags and toppings and other esoteric mysteries besides.

In the first few pages of this book Geoffrey Bucknall utterly dispels any mystique that may have grown up around fly dressing. He himself thinks he may even have offended a few self-appointed arch-priests, by demonstrating to so many ordinary people that no miracles are involved, that the most fumbling of fingers can become precision tools before long, and that good flies are actually tied by plain men not masterminds.

But he understands the trepidation of each and every beginner, and the sheer courage it takes to start on that first fly. He also understands the exasperation and frustration which accompany several flies thereafter, whilst those fumbling fingers continue to feel 'all thumbs'. And most important, he understands how to nurse you through this period – till processes that once seemed fiddly quite suddenly become automatic.

The author has every reason to understand all this – for he is in almost daily contact with beginners. For the last eight years he has run fly-tying classes in Peckham and in the City, and his classes are always full. His pupils past and present now number many hundreds (including several handicapped people to whom he has given special instruction) and their common comment is that he has 'opened up' an entire new world of fly fishing pleasure for them.

And they have taught him something in return, I believe. They have led him not only to remember continually what it is like to be a beginner, but also to know exactly which actions and processes a beginner finds most difficult – and how they can best be described and made simple.

This sympathy or empathy with beginners is what makes Geoffrey Bucknall a good teacher in print, as well as in person.

Contents

	Foreword by Dermot Wilson	v
	Acknowledgements	viii
1	Why Bother?	1
2	The Tools for the Job	4
3	Making a Simple Wet Fly	10
4	Making a Hackled Dry Fly	18
5	Making a Winged Wet Fly	24
6	Making a Split-Wing Dry Fly	31
7	Dressing Rolled-Wing Dry Flies	36
8	The Soft-Winged Wet Flies	39
9	How to Dress Mayflies	45
10	Nymphs and Beetles	52
11	The Use of Hair	57
12	Making Tube Flies	62
13	Dressing Low Water Flies	70
14	How to Make a Strip-Wing Salmon Fly and a Whole Feather-Wing Fly	76
15	How to Make Mixed-Wing and Built-Wing Salmon Flies	82
16	Modern Trends in Fly Dressing	89
	Book List	93
	Index	95

Acknowledgements

The author wishes to acknowledge the debt he owes to Mr. John Veniard, who was never too busy to help with welcome advice and information. He would also like to thank Keith Linsell and Ted Andrews for their drawings.

Finally, my thanks to Mr. Dermot Wilson for the kind sentiments in his Foreword.

1 Why Bother?

This simple question must be answered before I introduce you to the fascinating heraldry of fly dressing. I would not attempt to persuade you that the home-made fly is cheaper than a shop-bought one, but the angler who buys his own flies is a practical man; he purchases what he needs to catch fish. The amateur fly dresser is likely to be caught up in mystique of his art, and his spare funds will be devoted to serving it with endless permutations of material and technique. Fly dressing is an art in its own right, and I must present the perfectly-made artificial as a satisfaction in itself. Indeed, it may be so satisfying that its creator will not dare to cast it on the waters. It may go into a brooch, a frame or a glass paperweight, but never the jaw of a sharp-toothed trout. The comparison with heraldry is a good one, for fly dressing has its own vocabulary derived from an ancient ancestry.

It would be difficult to explain the collecting of coins, stamps, or even matchbox labels in purely logical terms. Fly dressing does score one point over these other fascinating pursuits, for it is both creative, and directed at a purpose, the catching of fish. I could defend the art as an occupation for long winter evenings, but to this I can add the importance of an angler making a fly to suit his own fishing tactics. The shop flies may have been heavily dressed with the display cabinet in mind, or the feathers employed may be too garish for the same reason.

On the other hand, the employee in the distant factory is unaware of the problems of your local stream or lake. How easy it is to collect a few samples of the insect life upon which the fish feed, then to fabricate copies in silk, fur and feather. It is easy, once you know how.

Why bother to make an artificial fly when there are so many natural insects to impale on the bare hook? The ancient Greeks must have asked themselves this same question, for the earliest flies we know of were made by them. The answer lies in the other aspect of fly fishing, the presentation of the fly. A natural insect, such as a Mayfly, can be dapped, or even floated downstream, but if an effort is made to drive it across the water with the action of the rod, it is thrown off the hook-point. From early times, anglers studied to make copies of these natural insects, and historically we find two threads of colour, red and black, running through many of the successful patterns.

When is a fly not a fly? When it is a fish! The artificial fly has developed to the extent that this name is given to any confection of silk, fur and feather that simulates an item of fish food. Thus it can be the silvery minnow fighting against the torrent, the unlikely pink prawn dodging through the salmon pool, or even the wriggling sandeel that stirs up the mackerel and cod. Nor need the dresser be confined to those traditional materials to tie to his hook-shank. Modern plastics introduce a whole range of shiny possibilities, which, in their turn, simplify many of the traditionally tricky operations. One notable example of this is the growing favour of the salmon fly dressed on a plastic tube instead of the old-fashioned meat-hook. All these modern innovations fall within my definition, for the processes of making them are done by hand. Above all, it is its alliance with the fly rod and tapered line that sets the seal on the name.

My purposes in this book are practical. I am anxious to show these processes of fly dressing so that they can be mastered in easy stages. I will outline the basic tools and materials. Since these processes and materials will place a wide range of artificials within reach of the reader, I shall not repeat here the thousands of patterns that may be dressed. Nor is the wide field of entomology involved, for although it is a pleasant, absorbing study that benefits the fly fisherman, basically the fly dresser is concerned with copying the size, colour and shape of the food on which the trout or other fish feed.

For example, the angler is dressing a hackled, dry Coachman for the first time. He is doing no such thing! He is dressing a hackled dry fly, and the pattern is quite unimportant. The processes are the things that matter, for by changing his materials, he could make any one of dozens of dry flies.

Nevertheless, even though I am a practical angler writing of a practical aspect of fishing, I must declare my underlying philosophy in fly dressing, for I am unashamedly Halfordian. I will explain this as doing my best to make an exact imitation of the fishes' food, within the limits of my craft and materials. F. M. Halford was a great fly fisherman around the turn of the century, who believed firmly in the doctrine of exact imitation. He took great pains to obtain exact size and colour in his artificials, but his school of thought came under fire. It is true that the messy dyeing procedures and opaque materials were later replaced by modern methods and translucent qualities, but this follows the same path. It was only time that passed Halford by; the doctrine was the same. If he was rightly accused of dogmatism, this is a fault of personality, from which we all suffer to a greater or lesser degree, and it has no bearing on his dictum. We have only to glance in a tackle catalogue to see the lists of flies bearing the name of Halford. They have stood the test that matters.

This book sprang from my experience in training people to dress their own flies in an evening class. At the outset, I discovered an interesting fact which made me cast my mind back to my own apprenticeship. The initial reaction to working with such tiny hooks and fine silks is to be discouraged, feeling 'all fingers and thumbs'. If one were teaching oneself at home, this is the most likely time for the project to be abandoned. The watering eyes and snapping threads lead to frustration and comments like: 'I shall never get the hang of this!'

Those who persevere discover that the fingers learn to work in miniature. I do not pretend to understand the physiology of this; I can only assure you that it does happen. Happily, I had a watchmaker in my group who assured everyone that after a week or two, the co-ordination between hand and eye becomes an automatic process, and the fingers exert the right pressure on the threads and feathers without conscious thought.

This then is fly dressing. It is an absorbing art in its own right, it serves the angler's practical needs, and it enables him to develop his personal tactics of fly fishing by copying the form and colour of the fishes' food in his local water. Also, as we shall see later, it assists him to copy its behaviour in or on the water.

I shall use the standard terms of 'wet' and 'dry' fly for those that sink or float. I shall avoid the division of flies into 'deceivers' and 'attractors' or 'flashers'. I believe that the taking of a fly by the fish is a reflex, and that the fly must be a good enough imitation of the food-form to trigger off that reflex. This is partly due to an efficient fly, partly due to its intelligent presentation and behaviour in or on the water. And that is all.

2 The Tools for the Job

In the chapters that follow, I shall describe the tools and materials that are used in fly dressing. My experience is that some dressers prefer to buy everything they need, while others delight in making all the tools as well as scrounging the feathers and wools from cushions and needlework baskets. I shall help both schools of thought. In the former case, my task is simple, for high-quality materials for fly dressers are supplied by Messrs. Veniard, and Tom Saville, who can cite generations of satisfied customers to support the claim.

The Vice

The basic tool we need is an efficient vice. If the budget is limited, it is a wise policy not to scrimp on this instrument. It is true that a primitive clamp is sometimes used, the jaws of which are tightened by means of a butterfly nut on a coarse thread. This will hold large hooks securely enough, but trout hooks tend to slip between the jaws, which are inevitably unsmooth. Furthermore, the bulk of this vice is an impediment. It is in the way of the hands when working with fine materials, and the materials cannot hang freely. With the possible exception of those working only with large salmon hooks, I would never recommend this type of vice.

This is the problem. The vice made for holding large hooks is unsuitable for small ones, and vice versa. There must be some compromise at the lower price. Of the cheaper vices, I have found that the model named 'Thornton' is adequate, while in the medium range, the 'Cranbrook' is excellent. The 'Salmo' is the Rolls-Royce of them all. The jaws of most fly vices are of the collet type, being tightened by a knurled screw. The cheaper models will securely hold hooks from the smallest trout size up to a size 4, and will thus accommodate the low-water salmon flies. The dearer ones, the 'Cranbrook' for example, will comfortably take a size 4/0 salmon hook, while the 'Salmo' will go up to 6/0.

No matter what pattern you select, the important thing is to choose one that holds the head of the vice well away from the stem, so that the hands can move freely above and below the hook. Other creature comforts include a rubber tension button, a clamp that allows the height of the vice to be adjustable, and, in the costlier models, a hinge where the head joins the stem to enable the hook to be held at a chosen angle. If the angle is fixed, I find it more comfortable to have the head at 45 degrees to the stem, and sometimes the stem can be bent to allow this. It goes without saying that the working parts should be inspected to ensure that they function, but the faces of the jaws must also be scrutinized for ridges which would prevent the hook from being held firmly. They must also mate perfectly.

The metalwork enthusiast will have no trouble in fashioning a suitable vice. Both the pin-vice head and the clamp can be bought separately in tool shops for a few shillings. They can be joined with a thick metal strip, which is then bent to the required angle.

Hand Tools

Hackle pliers are spring-loaded clips for the manipulation of small feathers as well as other materials. They come in three sizes, large, medium and small, in relation to the size of the flies for which they are to be used. These tools are so inexpensive that it is hardly worth the trouble to fabricate them. In practice, I have found considerable variation in the strength of their spring; test a few pairs, and select the strongest. Again, the jaws should be inspected for perfect matching. It is useful to have them in two sizes, the smallest, and the medium.

If hackle pliers have a fault, it is a tendency to sever the threads, tinsels, and feathers that they hold. If a slip of valve rubber is slid over one of the jaws it will prevent the fraying action.

Other items that must be bought are scissors. These are of the small, sharp-pointed surgical type, one pair having curved blades, the other straight. Again, it is foolish to economize – buy the best quality you can afford. Incidentally, a few razor-blades are worth their weight in gold, but for safety, should be held in a special holder, or be of the 'Eveready' type.

The 'dubbing'-needle is employed to varnish the heads of flies, and also to pick out the fibres of certain furs that have

5

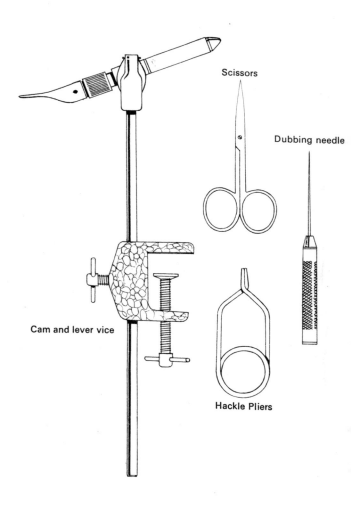

Scissors

Dubbing needle

Cam and lever vice

Hackle Pliers

Fig. 1. Some useful hand tools

been spun to the hook-shank. A long darning-needle pushed into a cork will fill all needs.

These are our basic requirements. There are also some special tools which I do not recommend – no doubt they are efficient, but it is my contention that we should not use tools for work that the fingers can do. This is not sheer sentiment for a 'handcraft'. One aspect of fly dressing is difficult to describe in words; it is the 'feel' that a pair of wings is settling down perfectly, that a turn of thread is tight enough. This 'feel' can only grow through the fingers, so the rule is never to hold a tool to a job that the fingers can do.

To be fair, I will briefly mention these tools. Firstly, there are winging pliers, which hold the wing slips in position while a turn or two of thread pulls them down to the hook-shank. In no other process is this subtle 'feel' so important as in winging, as we shall see later. Another tool performs the whip finish, which is also done easily by hand. Finally, a bobbin-holder will hold the spool of tying thread during dressing, keeping an even tension, and preventing the thread from being finger-soiled.

Tying in Comfort

Let us glance farther down the collection of tools that we have acquired. The fly dressing bench must be firm and of comfortable height. I find that an old bureau is most suitable. It is an excellent idea to pin a sheet of white board to the working surface, for this helps to reflect the light. The light itself should be strong, and adjustable, so that it shines on the work, but is masked from the eyes. An 'Anglepoise' table or reading lamp is good for this. Alternatively, the bench can be sited before a wide window, supposing that the fly dressing will be done in daylight hours.

These simple rules are most important, for although it is most relaxing to make a few flies on an otherwise cheerless winter's evening, a headache will soon ensue if the light is poor. What is worse, the flies will spoil. Eyesight is important in fly dressing, so it is a sensible precaution to have it checked before taking up our 'mini-craft'. Even though I considered my sight to be excellent, fly dressing once gave me headaches. On going to the optician, some errors were revealed and corrected, and my great pleasure was restored to me through a pair of thick horn-rims. Mr. Veniard does supply a pair of magnifying lenses, mounted as spectacles that sit on the end of the nose. One of our fly dressing group

7

at Peckham habitually brings the house down when he dons his pair, but the great trout that he takes out of the Test with his immaculate dry flies have never appreciated the joke!

A cabinet, or a number of boxes, will be required to hold all of the tools and materials. In either case, the containers must be airtight to protect the materials against moths. Cigar boxes are traditionally safe, as the tobacco is said to deter the would-be invaders.

These are the essentials. Personal choice may well range farther, into such frills as stands for the varnishes and paints. Those who choose to dye their own materials will need an old saucepan and strainer. I have also seen trays to hold hooks, the different sizes lying in separate compartments. There are metal shields, perforated with holes of varying diameters to slip over the head of the finished fly to protect the feathers when varnishing. A modern example of inventiveness is the fluorescence detector. This consists of a box, containing a tray for the fly, which is exposed to the sun's rays through a special screen at the top. The ultraviolet rays fall on the dressing, and the fluorescent materials are seen to shine through the eye-piece at the end of the box. Now that the 'Daylight' and D.F.M. materials are available, it is important that they be used sparingly in the dressings. This detector shows some alarming results, and the fish being sensitive to the ultra-violet end of the spectrum are also alarmed.

The fly hook itself is the most important link between angler and fish. It is a compromise between the fine wire needed to be as unobtrusive as possible, and light enough to float a dry-fly, with the strength and temper to hold a strong fish. You can trace complaints about fly hooks for at least five decades, probably longer.

Being somewhat critical of past hooks, I put in my own two cents' worth of design into my new 'Geoffrey Bucknall' fly hook, now widely sold. The manufacturer is the French firm of Viellard-Migeon where I spent a happy three days with their technicians in trying to achieve three factors – the elimination of the old ground point, which punctures like a needle but doesn't cut its way home, a short barb cut at only 10 per cent of the metal, and ridding the hook of the weakened tapered eye. All this was finally achieved within the format of the wide gape shape and forged bend. In fact the hook has proved itself in its first year as a strong hooker and holder of fish in standard length, while I go on to design the long shank version, for lures, streamers and bucktails.

In conclusion, having arranged the work-room with good light, firm bench and cabinet, the basic tool requirements are: an efficient vice; medium and small hackle pliers; sharp-pointed surgical scissors, curved and straight bladed; dubbing needle; razor blades. To which can be added if desired: whip-finish tool; winging pliers; bobbin holder; hackle guard; dye bath and strainer; magnifying spectacles; hook gauge, for measuring sizes of hooks; stand for varnishes; hook tray; fluorescence detector.

3 Making a Simple Wet Fly

Logically, a description of the necessary tools should be followed by a list of materials. The new-comer to fly dressing will be advised to begin with a small collection of furs and feathers to suit the simple, but popular flies of his choice. Around this nucleus, he will gradually build up his collection as his experience increases and a wider range of flies comes within his reach. Let this book follow the same course.

Obviously the first flies we dress will be the easiest ones. Let no one doubt that these first efforts will be effective. One of my own standbys for both stream and lake is a wet spider, employing two simple materials, and one dressing process. Above all, let us remember that the name of the pattern is unimportant at this stage. I stress the fact that the processes are the things to be mastered, and the whole complexity of fly names shall be temporarily shut out of the mind.

Given that an artificial fly is fashioned by attaching materials to a hook-shank, it will be evident that there are only two ways in which this can be done.

1. By fixing a material to the hook-shank so that it will be at an angle to the hook.

2. By fixing a material to the shank so that it lies parallel to the hook.

All fly dressing is based on these principles. An obvious example of the first principle is a body material that is wound round and round the hook-shank in even turns. A pair of wings lying on top of the hook-shank demonstrates the second rule.

Let us relate the first principle to a simple wet fly spider, the Black and Peacock.

Tying a Black and Peacock Spider

The first steps have already been mentioned, for the vice is set up on a firm bench with a white background, and the lighting is good. The tools are laid out to hand. A hook is securely tightened in the jaws of the vice, and given a good tweak to test its temper. It should spring back from this finger jerk to its original position. If it is soft, and bends easily, it is under-tempered, and should be discarded. If it is brittle through being over-tempered, it will simply snap. The hook should be gripped so that the lower bend is held firmly. I find it helps to mask the point of the hook in the jaws of the vice to prevent the tying thread from accidentally catching on it, for it will surely fray. Care must be taken with those hooks which are offset, for they snap readily if carelessly treated in the vice. Initially, the straight wide-bend hook is a sensible choice. Choose also a larger size to begin with, something like a size 10 (Redditch Old Scale).

You should decide to choose one hook scale, and stick to it. Since the Redditch scale is used more widely than the Cholmondeley-Pennell sizes, this is the one that I urge you to adopt. When you order hooks, be sure to indicate the scale, and remember that some varieties of make have a slightly different scale of sizes, such as the Model Perfect range. Hooks are another temptation for the economist, but a poorly-tempered hook that loses a fish makes for a poorly-tempered angler.

The varieties of hook are legion, as the catalogue will reveal, and it is wise to find a trusted pattern and stick to it. Hooks that I would recommend are the 'wide gape' variety of my own design, sold as 'Geoffrey Bucknall' fly hooks. These are trout hooks. It is also necessary to select a down-turned or up-turned eye. The down-eyed hook is vital for all trout wet flies and nymphs, for it acts like a miniature diving vane. It is unimportant which sort of eye is used on a dry fly, but these hooks are a finer wire than the wet fly ones, simply because they have to be kept afloat.

Having fixed the hook in the vice, the materials are selected and laid out near by. A tying thread of fine silk is needed to tie the materials to the hook-shank. For smaller trout flies, the grade known as 'Gossamer' is the one to use, and the black shade will match the dressing. The body will be of peacock herl, which must be bought for a few pence a packet, and the hackle is from the neck of a black hen. Hackles can be supplied through the dealer, or scrounged from friendly farmers or poulterers. The domestic hen supplies the downy, soft hackles for most wet flies, for a stiff hackle would impede the fly from sinking, or having a 'good entry' in fly fishing parlance.

The Tying Sequence

The first step is to wind the silk on to the hook-shank. A suitable length is broken from the reel; about 18 inches will suffice. The winding begins at a point a third of a shank along from the eye, and continues to just where the bend begins. The first turn must be made at an angle to the shank, so as to trap the loose end, but then the remaining even turns of silk are made at right angles to achieve a smooth bed of thread for the body material. This elementary step should be practised by itself until it can be performed perfectly. In learning the stages of our craft, you must school yourself to complete mastery of each one before proceeding to the next, and you must not accept anything short of perfection.

Having reached the hook-bend with the silk, you may nip it in the tension button on the vice, or alternatively clip on a pair of hackle pliers to prevent the thread from slipping, or coming unwound. At this stage, I should say that many dressers always wax their silks before winding, to assist them to stick to the shank, but if the process of winding is properly completed, it is not necessary to do this. Next, select two peacock herls. These should have a bronze colour, and if you examine them carefully, you will notice that the hairs, or 'flue' as we term it, are longer on one side of the quill. We want these longer hairs to stick upwards as the herl is wound on to the hook-shank. To accomplish this, the herls are tied in by their tips, together, so that the longer flue points to the rear of the hook. The herls are easily trapped against the underside of the shank by a couple of turns of tying silk, which is then wound back to its point of origin in even turns, binding down the stubs of herl.

The two herls are now wound together in the same way to the same point. A fine fuzzy body should result. If successful, the ends of the herl can again be trapped against the hook-shank by a few turns of silk, and the roots trimmed away by scissors or blade. An alternative way to make a peacock herl body is to tie in four herls, twisting them together before making the body. It does not make quite such a fuzzy effect as the former method.

The hackle must now be tied in to make the legs of our spider. Select a big hackle, and strip away the fluffy fibres at the root, so that about an inch of stalk is left bare. Trap this against the underside of the hook, using the turns of silk in the form of a figure-of-eight to keep the feather up-

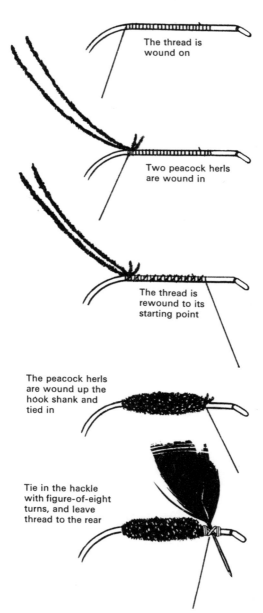

The thread is
wound on

Two peacock herls
are wound in

The thread is
rewound to its
starting point

The peacock herls
are wound up the
hook shank and
tied in

Tie in the hackle
with figure-of-eight
turns, and leave
thread to the rear

Fig. 2. Tying a Black and Peacock Spider

right, and at right angles to the hook. Once you realize that the hackle fibres have to stand out from the hook as the feather is wound round the shank, it will be obvious why I recommend this method of tying it in. Now pass the thread towards the rear of the hook, keeping it taut meanwhile. The hackle pliers are clipped on to the tip of the feather, which is given two turns round the hook-shank. Care must be taken to ensure that the turns are straight, so that the fibres spring away at right angles to the hook. The winding should be so that the end of the feather is at the rear of the hackle fibres, where it can be easily trapped by a turn of thread, then trimmed away.

The thread is carefully worked through the fibres, so that its turns bind the stalk securely to the shank. A few turns are now made to build up the head of the fly, which is then finished by whip-turns.

The Whip Finish

Although a fly can be completed with a few half-hitches, the dressing will certainly come undone. It is vital to master the whip-finish, which speedily and surely keeps all your handiwork in its right place. Once it is understood in theory, the practical movements can be applied. A whip-finish is simply a loop binding down on its loose end, which is then pulled tight through the turns of the binding. In other words, if you make a loop in the thread, then run it down on top of the hook-shank, it is possible to take hold of the tight side of the loop and wind it round the hook-shank over the loose end of silk. Then, holding the turns firmly between your fingers, so that they do not slip, the end of the thread is pulled until the knot is tight.

Alternatively, you may buy the tool, complete with instructions, that does exactly the same thing for you. But lest this confuses you, follow these simple rules and illustrations, and you will succeed:

1. Make a simple loop.
2. Run it down on to the hook-shank.
3. Take hold of the 'tight' side of the loop, bind it down with two or three turns over the 'loose' side.
4. Holding the turns firmly, with the free hand, pull the end of the silk tightly through the knot you have made.
5. Trim off loose end of silk.

Fig. 3. A whip finish

It only needs a drop of clear cellulose varnish on the head of the fly, and it is ready to go trouting.

Having made a Black and Peacock Spider for the first time, let us consider some of the lessons. Firstly, it is important to leave enough room between the eye of the hook and the hackle. The point at which the thread is first wound in marks the limit of the body. If this is gauged correctly – about a third of the way along the shank from the eye -- it leaves enough room for the hackle and the head, and the knot of the angler's cast.

Variations on a Theme

What is in a name? By simply switching the body and hackle colours, dozens of deadly patterns are already available. Let us collect a few more materials to fill the armoury.

A spool of orange silk and a dozen brown partridge hackles give us the Orange Partridge. Yellow silk with this hackle is equally effective on lake or stream. A brown silk body with the black hen hackle gives us Stewart's favourite Black Spider, while black silk to match the same hackle gives us the more orthodox dressing. I could go on, but why should I spoil the pleasure of your voyage of discovery? Search them out.

Already you can add that personal style I mentioned. These sparsely-hackled spiders, for you must never exceed two turns of hackle, are first-rate on fast moorland becks. A turn or two of silk behind the hackle makes it flare out; dressing the fly with a 'kick' we call it. The upstream cast is not ruined by the current forcing the fibres into invisibility by clinging against the body. They dance in the stream.

Equally, the bodies may be made chubby by tying in a length of floss silk to make an underbody before the herl is wound on. Here are the beetle and water-bug outlines, especially effective in lakes. A quickly-sinking fly to scour the bottom in cold water is easily made by winding a layer of 5-amp. fuse wire on to the hook-shank before you fashion the body. There are many variations on the original theme.

Checklist of Materials

Here is a summary of our needs for these first steps in fly dressing, making the simple wet fly spiders.

1. Gossamer tying silks in several colours; black, yellow, orange, brown

2. Herls for bodies; bronze peacock, ostrich dyed green, brown and black.

3. Hen hackles; black, brown, olive, etc.

4. Brown partridge hackles, or from grouse, snipe, or woodcock.

5. Clear cellulose varnish.

4 Making a Hackled Dry Fly

Hackles

A dry fly is one that floats; it floats because the hackles are stiff enough to support the weight of the fly on the skin of the water. Its purpose is to copy flies that have just hatched, those that have returned to the water on egg-laying missions, those that have died and are being swept away downstream, known as the spent gnats, and finally, luckless creatures such as moths and daddy-long-legs that have carelessly blundered into the water and cannot escape. The field is enormous, but it depends on that certain quality of hackle, steely and bright.

These hackles come from the cockerel, but he must have been scratching around the range for three years or so for the fibres to be really strong. The modern methods of broiler production, intensive farming and wet plucking makes it increasingly hard to find quality 'capes', as the necks of feathers still on the skin are known. Naturally they are more expensive as the shortage becomes more acute. Some of the most important colours come from rare breeds. The inky shade we call 'Iron Blue' is from the Andalusian breed, rapidly dying out, and a cape from such a cockerel is almost priceless. In fact, many of our hackles are imported, while the rare colours are dyed. Fortunately, we do not lose the quality so much as they used to in earlier times, when dyeing also degreased the feathers considerably. We are also finding ways of making do with poorer quality hackles.

Tying a Hackle

Let us make a simple pattern, using one body material, and one hackle. We will not put a name to the fly, but simply master the processes of making it. The hook will be a size 12, light in wire, and we will make our body as before, from two peacock herls. Having reached this stage, it is only necessary to add the hackle.

This hackle is brown, with a reddish tinge. They are quite easy to come by since they are taken from the more popular Rhode Island breed. It is not sufficient to take any

18

hackle at random from the neck or packet. One must be carefully chosen to match the hook size, for should it be too long, the fly will be held too far above the water for the fishes comfort, while short fibres will not allow it to cock up cheekily as in the classic tradition. For a size 12 hook, a hackle of roughly between an inch and an inch and a half will be most suitable, but since fibres vary in length, the hackle should be bent round the hook-bend. If the fibres are of correct length, they should extend to the hook-eye. One curiosity about hackles is that the fibres are of uniform length from tip to root.

The fluffy fibres at the root are stripped away to leave the stem bare, and the hackle is bound in with the same figure-of-eight tying. The silk is held to the rear, while the hackle is carefully wound in at right angles to the hook. In a dry fly, more turns are needed than in the spider wet fly, but the temptation to overhackle the fly must be resisted. Four to five turns are adequate. After this, you merely add to the weight of the fly and defeat your own object. Besides, the amount of hackle should never be enough to offer a mass of resistance to the flow of water. The water must be free to move between the points or else the shape of the fly is ruined. Then the surplus fibres have to be cut out with scissors, and the others revived in the steam from the spout of a kettle of boiling water.

After the hackle has been done, the silk is wound back through the fibres, being careful not to trap them. A backwards and forwards movement with the thread will allow

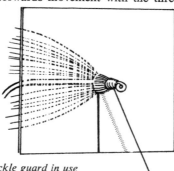

Fig. 4. A hackle guard in use

these fibres to spring clear. Finally, the head is made, whip-finished, and varnished. It is a good idea to make a small cap of thin cardboard, with a hole in the middle, and a slit to the edge. This is slipped over the head of the fly to pull the hackle clear of the varnish, and, if you wish, the whip-finish, for the silk is easily passed forward through the slit in the cap.

The process is a slight extension of the earlier one for the wet fly, and this also enlarges the dresser's scope by dozens of patterns. To take advantage of these, it is now necessary to examine further the selection of hackles. These may be bought on the neck as a cape, in large packets containing hundreds of feathers, or in small cellophane envelopes of a dozen chosen to suit the size of hook. It is obviously cheaper in the long run to buy the larger quantity.

A Selection of Hackles

Some colours of hackle are straightforward enough. The natural black, white, ginger, and medium, light and dark reds, are immediately recognizable, whilst the dyed colours, such as olive, orange, or blue are quite straightforward at first sight. The situation is complicated by shades of these colours. Olive subdivides into green olive, golden olive, brown olive as well as medium, light and dark olive; nor is orange to be confused with that most important fly dressing colour, hot orange. A simple way out of that dilemma is to buy a chart which has the dyed hackles placed against the correct name of colour and shade.

The next problem is to unravel the tangled skein of the special names that fly dressers have inherited from the past. These describe certain selected colours of hackles, some of which have more than one colour in their make up. (You will recall my reference to our 'heraldry'.) I will list the most important of these names, and describe the colour of the hackle concerned.

Dun – a mousy colour.
Blue Dun – a smoky-grey colour.
Iron Blue – a dark blue, inky colour.
Badger – a white hackle with black roots.
Greenwell – ginger hackle with black roots.
Furnace – red hackle with black roots.
Coch-y-bondhu – as above, but with black tips.
Grizzle – black and white barred hackles.
Honey Dun – honey-coloured with dark roots.
Rusty – dark hackles flecked with 'rust'.

The derivations from these names, Honey Blue Dun, Brassy Badger, Rusty Blue Dun describe very rare colours, but they are explicable from the above table.

Once again, the commonsense approach is to obtain a selection of cock hackles in colours that are most likely to serve immediate needs, and to expand stocks as required. To relate this to simple hackled dry flies, it is necessary to turn again to the fly we have just made. To make this into a recognizable pattern, would be simply a matter of adding a white cock's hackle. This could either be mixed with the natural red hackle by winding the two in simultaneously, or by using a short red hackle in front of a longer white one. This tells us of two important capes to buy, the natural red one, which is in reality a reddish-brown, and a white one. Other useful capes are of medium olive, black and blue dun, though these may well be dyed.

With the technique of winding a hackle fresh in the mind, let us examine ways to overcome the problems of poor quality and rare colours. I have explained the reason for matching size of hackle to hook, but it is obvious that a long hackle can be carefully clipped back to the right size. The appearance of the fly is heavy-footed, but the result is a better floater, and even feathers from the young birds can be treated in this way.

A glance at the list of bi-coloured hackles shows that they have one thing in common. The roots are all of dark hue, usually black. The feathers that match the tips of the hackles are still obtainable, and cheaper. Is it possible to turn a ginger hackle into a Greenwell by darkening the root? I have successfully applied Indian ink with a brush, or magic marker, while an even more effective substitute has been suggested by John Veniard. This is to wind a black ostrich herl through the hackles after they have been wound in. This makes a clearly visible dark centre to the fly, suggestive of the thorax of the natural insect.

Many of the body materials for dry flies have already been collected. For example, the peacock herls provide for the Coachman and the Coch-y-bondhu, while the silks form the bodies for such flies as the Greenwell and the Medium Olive. By another simple process, the family of flies known as the 'Quills' are drawn into our orbit. The bodies for these artificials are formed from the peacock herl that has been stripped of its flue.

Such a fly is the Ginger Quill. Let us dress this fly, incorporating tail whisks.

Tying a Ginger Quill

The silk is wound in. It is even more important to have a smooth bed for this delicate body, and the thread must be

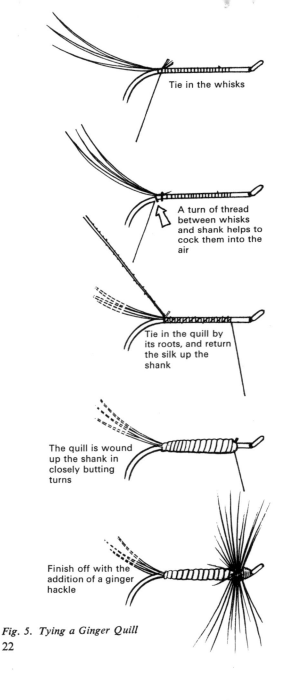

Tie in the whisks

A turn of thread between whisks and shank helps to cock them into the air

Tie in the quill by its roots, and return the silk up the shank

The quill is wound up the shank in closely butting turns

Finish off with the addition of a ginger hackle

Fig. 5. Tying a Ginger Quill

22

chosen to resemble the colour of the hackle. The whisks are a small bunch of fibres torn from a spade hackle to match the legs. There are always some of these longer feathers in each cape. The fibres are held on top of the hook while a loop of the silk is passed over them, then carefully pulled tight. No more than two turns should be used in this business, or there will be an unsightly bulge at the end of the hook. The roots of the fibres may be twitched away, or bound down beneath the body. When you are satisfied that they are sitting correctly on top of the shank, pass a further turn between them and the shank to cock them up into the air, as in the natural insects you spot by the riverside.

While the tension is maintained on the silk by hackle pliers or rubber button, carefully strip the flue from a herl by drawing it between the finger-nails. These herls are extremely fragile, but if the flue is pulled gently downwards, it soon flakes away. You will notice that the bare quill is pale ginger at the bottom, turning to a rich chocolate-brown higher up. It is the lighter shade that we need for this fly, so the herl is tied in by the root, and carefully wound after the thread towards the hook-eye. This is best done by hand, for the jaws of the hackle pliers soon fracture the quill, and destroy the 'feel' of the right pressure. The turns of quill must butt up against each other, and not overlap, or leave gaps between turns. At the end of the body, the quill is tied off, twitched away, and a ginger hackle wound in.

The use of matching quills and hackles makes a wide range of flies. We shall meet the dye-pot later; it is sufficient to note here that if hackles and quills are dyed at the same time, the shades of orange, red, blue, and cinnamon will match perfectly.

Having placed so many flies within reach, let us add the necessary materials to our collection:

Cock capes in the following colours:
White, black, medium red, dyed olive and blue dun.
Gossamer silks in olive, red and grey.

5 Making a Winged Wet Fly

I will make no bones about it, this is the hump of fly dressing. Once you are over the trouble of 'winging', it is all downhill, but since you may not dodge it, it is as well to analyse the difficulties and find ways to overcome them. Basically, it is continual practice, for there are no short cuts. The aim is to match two slips of feather, then pull them down on top of the hook-shank by means of the tying thread. In short, this is to follow the second of the principles I mentioned in Chapter 3 -- that of fixing a material to the hook-shank so as to lie parallel to it.

The two main faults that beset us are the tendency for the wings to twist round the hook-shank with the pressure of the thread, and the likelihood of the fibres of the wings to fly apart.

At the outset, it must be realized that some feathers are easier to use than others. Strong feathers from the wings of starling and duck are less prone to splitting than soft feathers such as the barred flank ones from teal and mallard. It is sensible to start with these stouter plumages.

There is yet another precaution that we should take in advance to save frustration. Feathers have a natural oil, but they dry out after plucking. Dry feathers are murder to work with, so the answer is to buy or find fresh feathers in small quantities that will soon be used. These wings are also subject to attack by moth and feather mite, and must therefore be stored in airtight containers, sprinkled inside with camphor or naphtha flakes.

Tying a Greenwell's Glory

The drill for dressing a standard winged wet fly, such as that drab little killer, the Greenwell's Glory, will introduce us to some fascinating new problems. The tying silk starts off as primrose yellow, but it is well waxed in beeswax until it turns to a dirty olive shade. Strangely, it takes on a vaguely translucent appearance when wet. This silk thread is wound on to the hook-shank in the usual way, and when the hook-bend is reached, the whisks may be added if required.

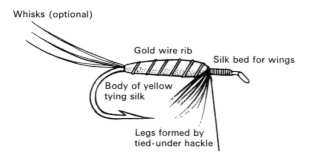

Fig. 6. Greenwell's Glory, ready for winging

The next step is to tie in a short length of gold wire for a ribbing. This has two purposes. It adds a subtle flash to the fly, but it also protects the silk from the teeth of the fish. It is trapped against the underside of the hook-shank by a turn of thread, and it is helpful to make a slight kink in the wire at that point to key it to the silk. The spare end of wire can be bound down as the silk is wound evenly back to the end of the body. The wire is then ribbed over the silk in diagonally-spiralled turns. Be warned! The even spacing of these spirals is one of the acid tests of a competent dresser. The wire is tied down firmly at the end of the body, and the spare end clipped off.

Although the Greenwell has a hackle named in its honour, the more usual Furnace hen supplies the legs. To begin with, the hackle is formed in the usual way, but when the silk is brought forward, the fibres are divided on top of the hook into two equal parts, both of which are pulled downwards below the shank, and held in this position by two or three diagonal turns of thread. This is facilitated if the fibres are thoroughly moistened with saliva; spit is one free aid to fly dressing. I have found it a good scheme to cut out the few hackle fibres in the centre on top of the hook before I divide them.

Preparing for Winging

This leaves a slight hump on top of the shank, and between this and the eye there should remain enough space to accommodate the wings. The wings must bed down on silk, like debutantes, for the bare hook-shank is both too narrow and too shiny for their support. At the same time, if the wings are to lie close to the body of the fly, this silk bed must be built up to the same level as the hump, for it would otherwise cock them upwards. This is a minor point governing style. Having prepared a comfortable bed for the wings, the thread can be slipped over the rubber tension-button while the slips are prepared.

These wing slips are taken from opposing primary feathers from a starling's wing. The general colour is grey, but the fastidious dresser might care to select his wings from the dealer's stock, for individual feathers vary considerably according to the age of the bird and the season. Younger birds, and those killed early in the season usually provide lighter shades, while darker wings come from the older birds. The primary feathers are those long ones that give the wing its sweep. The secondaries are the shorter feathers in the middle of the wing, but the fluffy ones along the 'leading' edge are known as the coverts, many of which make fine hackles.

Two primary feathers are selected, one from each wing, and a small slip marked out with the point of the scissors towards the middle. The actual width of each section is a matter of taste, although they should match. Some six to eight fibres is a rough guide for a medium wing. The two slips can be carefully detached from their parent feathers, either with the scissors, or, for the brave, by boldly twitching them out between the fingers. Practise with a spare feather. Either way, it may well be that one or two fibres may split away. In nature, the fibres are locked together by other microscopic fibres down each side, and it is possible to remarry them by stroking them gently in the same direction as the sweep of the feather.

Winging

Having matched the wing slips successfully, they have to be put together to make a pair. In a wet fly, the natural curve is towards the hook; in other words the slips are pressed face to face. It is then up to the dresser whether he chooses the fly to have upswept or down-curved wings, though the latter style is more popular in trout patterns. Now it only remains to fix the paired wing slips to the hook. I will break this down into separate stages.

1. Hold the wings by their tips between the finger and thumb of the left hand on the top of the hook-shank in the desired position.
2. Make a loop of thread over the wings, and hold the loop with the wings through them with the left hand.

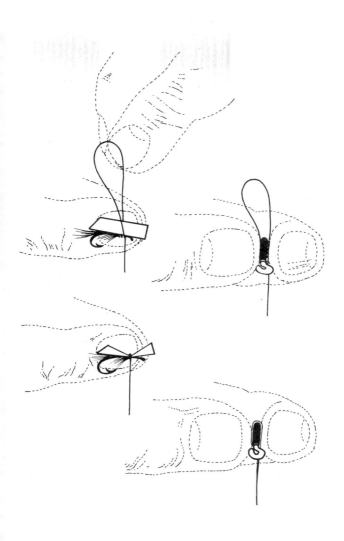

Fig. 7. Winging a Greenwell's Glory

3. Still holding the loop with the wing slips through it, pull the silk tightly, so that the wings are brought down on top of the hook-shank.

4. Before you release the grip on the wings, make another two turns of the silk immediately to the right of the first turn.

If this has been successful, when the wings are released they should be sitting perfectly on top of the hook, in line with the shank. What has happened is this. The loop of thread has pulled each fibre down on to the one below it, like a concertina. The purpose of the finger grip is to prevent the fibres acting in any other fashion, as well as to position the wings correctly. If a simple turn were made over the wings instead of this, the fibres would slide down on each side, the wings would flatten and break.

There are some secrets to perfect winging. It is vital to keep an even tension on the thread during the whole process. Should the subsequent turns of silk be tighter than the first one, the wings will be twisted around the hook. One way of guarding against this is by performing a whip-finish as soon as the wings are released. It is also important to ensure that the turns of silk move from left to right, towards the eye of the hook, to prevent a flattening of the wings, as well as an unsightly bump at the head of the fly. Finally, the wing slips must be held closely to the hook-shank, and the loop must be pulled down in a straight line.

In 1966 I was one of a team demonstrating fly dressing at the National Angling Exhibition. Of all the questions fired at me, 'Can you show me correct winging?' was the most common. You will not succeed the first time. I advise you to practise on a spare hook without the body. Do you remember the days when you were learning to skate, or ride a bicycle? You kept toppling over until you thought it was all against Nature. Then, quite suddenly, it came. Winging is like that, and once acquired, the habit lasts a lifetime. It depends on this mysterious 'feel' that slowly develops without conscious awareness. This is why I counsel perseverance without the aid of special tools or inventive ways of doing the job.

There is one last process to do. The roots of the wings have to be trimmed away. If these stubs are raised, and the scissors held flat along the shank, when they are cut away, a taper is left, which, when evenly bound with the silk, makes a delicately-shaped head for the fly. Once again, we have not so much made a Greenwell as any one of dozens of flies by choosing the appropriate wing, body, and tail materials, not forgetting a silver or gold ribbing.

Materials

This might be a good point to adjourn proceedings to consider how to know what materials to collect. As in chess, we have an intelligible code for expressing the moves required. For instance, in a manual of dressings, our Greenwell would be listed as follows:

Hook – size 12 (old scale).
Body – yellow silk, well waxed.
Rib – gold wire.
Hackle – furnace hen.
Wing – starling.

By looking up the favourite patterns, you will be able to discover the materials you need to add to your collection. I must sound a note of caution here. The wings of most of our artificials are of three colours, either brown, white or grey. The inventors of the patterns used materials that were convenient to their area; thus there has been much duplication, which has been inherited by us. We need only to know the colour, and not clutter up our cabinets with many rare feathers that will scarcely be used. This is shown by the use of starling in the Greenwell, for the originator, Canon Greenwell wrote in his own fair hand: 'inside of a blackbird's wing'. Not only is this bird protected, but the colour is too similar to starling to warrant a quibble. The answer is to concentrate on the principal colours at this stage.

This situation can be more simplified. The lake flies are recognized by their names, which show the wing material with the body colour, such as the Grouse and Green. There are also the Mallard and Green and the Woodcock and Green. These flies are too similar to require duplication in the fly box, so it is only necessary to select one wing feather to suit the whole range. This is done by personal taste, my own being the 'grouse' series.

Apply this logic to the body materials, for once again the colours may be represented by floss silk, seal's fur, wool, or one of the modern polymer dubbings. My own preference is for seal's fur, for it has a straggly appearance which reflects points of light, whereas the others are smooth. We shall learn shortly how the wools and furs are twirled round the shank to make a coloured body.

I now summarize the materials to collect for the cabinet to bring this vast range of wet fly patterns within reach.

Hen hackles, in various colours.
Grey wings: starling or duck.
Brown wings: hen, woodcock or grouse.
White wings: swan or duck.
Body materials in white, black, green, red, claret, olive, brown and hot orange: seal's fur, wool or floss silk.
A spool of gold wire.
A spool of fine silver tinsel.
Golden pheasant tippet feathers for tails.

6 Making a Split-Wing Dry Fly

We have now come to the cream of fly dressing, for without a doubt the correctly-tied, split-wing dry fly is the most beautiful example of the fly dresser's art. Perhaps one of the reasons why the simple hackle fly is widely preferred is the time and patience required to master the processes. There is little doubt in my mind that the addition of a pair of wings represents more exactly the natural fly, particularly at the moment when it has just alighted on the water, for these same wings act like a parachute, slowing down the fly's descent and helping it to land the right way up. I will extol its virtues no longer, but analyse its structure.

Tying a Blue Dun

One fly that traces its family tree back to the days of Izaak Walton, and beyond, is the Blue Dun. It also intro-

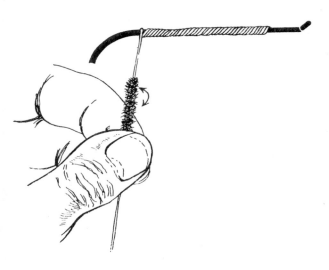

Fig. 8. Fur spun to silk

31

duces us to yet another stage of fly tying, that of dubbing a body fur for the body. The fur in question comes from the pelt of a mole.

The fly is an exception in another way, for the silk does not match the blue colour of the body and hackle. It is primrose yellow, and the effect of the fly is obtained by using the fur sparingly, so that the yellow silk shines through it when wet. The silk is wound down towards the bend, the tail whisks from a large blue dun cock's hackle are tied in, and a pinch of mole's fur is spun on to the silk, close to the hook-shank.

To start with, the silk must be well waxed at this point so that the fur will adhere to it. The fur is teased out and spun round the silk between the finger and thumb of the left hand, while the right hand keeps the silk taut. This rolling action must be in one direction only, otherwise the fur is unwound as fast as it is spun on the silk. The silk and fur are now wound round the shank to form the body over two thirds of the hook's length. Immediately in front of this blue body, two layers of silk make a bed for the wings.

In the case of this dry fly, the hackle is wound in after the wings have been completed. The next task is the selection of wing slips as before, from the opposing primary wing-feathers of a starling. However, when these slips are matched together, they must curve outwards, unlike those in the wet fly. In other words, they are back to back.

They are fixed to the top of the hook-shank in exactly the same way as in the Greenwell, but when the slips are secured with a whip-finish, and the ends trimmed away, they have to be raised into the vertical position and divided. Firstly, a turn of silk is taken around the base of the wings. Then they are carefully parted with the dubbing-needle while a figure-of-eight is made between them with the silk. This keeps them permanently divided, and subtle variation in the pressure applied to the thread will govern the flare of the wings. In all winging processes, I cannot too strongly emphasize that the secret of success lies in the careful gauging of the right pressure to apply to the thread. This should neither be loose, nor yet as tight as the thread will stand without breaking. I call to mind the fencing master's command to hold the sword as one would grasp a captive bird, neither so slack that it can wriggle free, nor so tight as it will give injury. Substitute a live fish and you will learn my meaning.

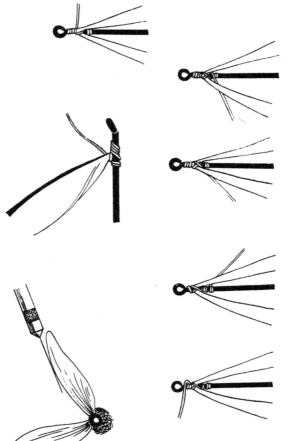

Fig. 9. Making split wings

The Hackle

If the wings have divided well, take two more turns of thread forward for nipping in the hackle. This is also of the blue dun shade, the size being judged as described previously. The fluffy base-fibres are stripped away, and the hackle tied in front of the wings. I make two turns in front of the wings, and the remaining three close behind them to lend support. The thread, which had been held to the rear, ties down the spare tip, which is twitched away, wound through the hackle, under the wings, and forms the head and whip-finish. The hackle stalk is cut away, the head varnished, and there you are.

Some dressers tie in two separate hackles, one in front of the wings, the other behind. I have explained that over-hackling does nothing for the fly except add to the weight and the cost. Some dressers also cut away the stalk from the hackle as soon as it is tied in, but as, in my experience, it takes time for a new dresser to adjust himself to the pressure to apply when winding, there is a danger of the hackle being tugged out. One frustration leads to another. In the winging, we are able to select a style by the curve of the feathers. It is more usual to have them sweeping up towards the hook-eye. During the process, particularly with old feathers, one or two fibres may detach themselves from their companions. Gently stroking them should make them remarry, and a diluted speck of varnish can anoint the wing-tips to keep them together.

The Advanced Wing Style

It is also evident that a fly may be winged in reverse, so that the wings spread out over the eye of the hook. This is the advanced wing style as used in the 'Variant' dry flies. The winging processes are exactly the same, except that the slips are held the 'wrong way round' to begin with; that is to say, the tips point to the right, over the eye of the hook. Variants have small, slim wings, while the hackles are sparse and longer than usual. The effect is spidery. Finally, the Variant's wings are completely varnished.

To assist the dry fly to float, the angler usually souses it in a silicone solution at the water's edge. The dresser may treat his fly at home, and in spite of the modern water-proofing compounds, I have found nothing to beat the ancient practice of steeping the fly in paraffin, then allowing it to dry out on a window-ledge. The result is a fly that floats well and keeps the moths at bay. A final thought is to run the point of a needle through the eye, just in case a drop of varnish has sealed it.

Now let us add a few more items to our collection, such as some bi-coloured hackles. Badger and Furnace are useful, while some starling wings dyed Iron Blue will surely be required for the ubiquitous fly that bears that name.

These last two chapters cover the most difficult stages of fly dressing. I reiterate that practice is the key to success. Coupled with this, the dresser must never content himself with anything short of a perfect finish, for if one stage is imperfect, it will ruin the next as surely as night follows day.

7 Dressing Rolled-Wing Dry Flies

There are some natural flies whose wings lie flat in repose, often extending well beyond the body. These are the sedges, moths, stoneflies and the alder. To copy these the dresser uses a 'rolled' wing, perhaps the easiest of all of our methods of making wings. It also gives us the opportunity of learning how to make a 'palmered' hackle, which crops up in its own right in such patterns as the Zulu, Blue Zulu and Red Palmer. Both these stages are incorporated in the preparation of the Cinnamon Sedge, surely one of the most killing patterns in summer on stream or lake.

Tying a Cinnamon Sedge

The hook, size 12, is firmly fixed in the vice, and the orange gossamer silk is evenly lapped down towards the hook-bend. At this point, a short length of gold wire is tied in for a ribbing, together with three or four fibres of either cinnamon-coloured turkey tail, or the reddish fibres from the long feathers from the centre of a cock pheasant's tail. These are easily cadged from the butcher at Christmas time.

The silk is wound back to the head, and the body formed by even turns of these fibres, which are nipped under the shank by the thread and the spare ends trimmed away. It is important to leave ample room for the wings and two hackles between the end of the body and the hook-eye. Next, a reddish-brown hackle (Rhode Island) from a cockerel is tied in at the throat. This hackle should be of good length, say one and a half inches, for it is now wound down the body in diagonal turns to the tail, where it is left hanging by the weight of the hackle pliers. Care must be taken to see that the turns are evenly spaced, and that the hackle fibres spring out at an angle from the body. The wire is now spiralled up the body, over the hackle, thus binding it down securely. Again, care must be exercised to ensure evenly-spaced spirals, while bunches of hackle that are trapped or pulled out of position, can be freed by the dubbing-needle.

The hackle tip is clipped away, as is the spare end of wire after it has been lashed down.

The Rolled Wing

A bed of silk is prepared for the wings in the usual way. The wing section is taken from a single feather. The colour should be a splotchy brown, and candidates include light brown hen and brown owl. The formerly popular

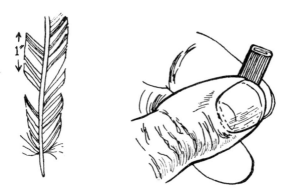

Fig. 10. Taking out a section, and rolling the wings

'Landrail' is virtually unobtainable, I believe, due to the bird protection laws, which few will rail at, if you will excuse the dreadful pun. Substitutes are obtainable from houses like Veniard, but the feathers I mention will suffice, of which owl is a personal favourite.

A section of the middle feather, which should be a primary, is taken out with the scissors so that it measures about an inch long. It is simply rolled up like a carpet, and the base of the roll is squeezed between the finger and thumb of the left hand. It is then pulled down to its bed on top of the hook-shank in the usual way. There should result a low, flat wing section which divides automatically, although this has to be done sometimes with the point of the dubbing-needle. The wing should also extend beyond the hook-bend, as in the natural fly.

When the roots of the wings have been snipped off, a further reddish hackle is tied in, and wound in over the throat, disguising the untidy ends. The thread secures this hackle in the customary way, and the head is completed and varnished.

These processes are used on many flies, including the whole of the sedge family, numbering more than a dozen. I can call to mind the Silverhorns, the Silver Sedge, the Little Red Sedge and the Dark Sedge to give an idea of its scope. To this, you may add the moths, such as the Hoolet, put up on large hooks with long shanks, which possibly need a sliver of cork lashed under the body to assist buoyancy. There is that popular fly, the Alder, and the wet Invicta which may be dressed in this way. Let us collect a few more materials in readiness:

A pair of brown owl wings for the moths.

Brown hen for the sedges.

Dark freckled hen wings for the Alder, and some peacock herl, dyed maroon, for its body.

A hen pheasant tail for the wings of the Invicta, and some blue jay hackles for its legs.

A cock pheasant's centre tail feather for the body of the Cinnamon Sedge.

And do not forget the mothballs!

8 The Soft-Winged Wet Flies

Mallard and Teal Feathers

This group of flies is treated separately, for although the techniques of winging are basically similar to those already described, there are some difficulties due to the fragility of the feathers. These are the barred feathers from the flanks of the mallard and teal, the former being of an attractive bronze hue, while the teal is simply black and white, like a bull's-eye. Both come in shades varying from dark to light, and it is important to remember this, for some patterns stipulate a 'dark teal' for example. There is one other point to bear in mind. These feathers are so popular for winging that many dressers forget that both birds provide many other plumages for flies. They forget to stipulate that they require the flank feathers when they order materials, and when they ask for 'mallard wings', the dealer sends them just that!

To avoid confusion, it is a sensible precaution to mention the name and size of the fly you intend to dress when you order. The dealer will see that you have what you need. In case you think that I am making a fuss about very little, I will outline some of the materials that the two ducks yield. The small brown mallard feathers for trout-sized flies actually come from the shoulder of the bird. The breast provides grey feathers, as does the real flank, and these are used in their natural state, or dyed for the fan-wings of Mayflies, as we shall see later. The quill-feathers from the wings, as the primaries are called, are of a light, slaty grey. They are excellent for the wings of such flies as the Wickham, and can be used as an alternative to starling wings, particularly when a stouter feather is called for, as in the larger Greenwell, or for fast water. The blue 'secondaries' are famous for the Butcher series of wet flies, while the white-tipped sections of them are for the Heckhams.

The same situation exists for teal. As the word 'wing' readily springs to mind when writing the order, I suggest you fall into the routine of making out the form like this:

1 dozen mallard shoulder feather for size 12 Mallard and Claret.

1 dozen light teal flank feathers for size 12 Peter Ross.

There are other fragile feathers besides the ones mentioned, such as barred widgeon, but the problems are the same. Generally speaking, the quilled feathers from the wings and tails of birds are stronger and easier to manipulate than body feathers, from flanks, shoulders or breasts. Since I have already nominated two patterns that figure very strongly in the fly fisherman's repertoire, the Mallard and Claret, and the Peter Ross, let us examine the problems that crop up in dressing them.

Tying a Mallard and Claret

To deal with them in order, having fixed a hook in the vice, tested it, and run on the silk, the next step is to tie in the tail. This consists of a bunch of tippet feathers from the neck of a golden pheasant. This form of tail is so widely used in flies for sea trout as well as in lakes and reservoirs, that it is simply known as 'tippet'. The trick is to tie them in so that all the fibres are equal, for they are of a bright orange colour with a black bar and tips, which should coincide. I find the best way to achieve this effect is to pull down a bunch of the feathers, binding them down to the hook before cutting them from the parent feather.

The next stage is to tie the ribbing under the shank. This is a length of gold wire or fine oval tinsel. Then the dubbing is prepared. Normally, this would consist of claret seal's fur, but over the years, experience shows that this fly is more successful if the fur is darkened. If we mix in a pinch of mole's fur with the seal, we darken it, and the softer texture of the mole makes the dubbing to the silk much easier. The mixing is easily accomplished if the furs are teased out, then worked together with the needle. The mixture is spun to the silk, making it slightly thicker towards the base in order to make a cigar-shaped taper on the body of the fly. The body is formed, and the ribbing is then spiralled up the body in the opposite direction to avoid the wire burying between the turns of the dubbing. In short, the dubbing is wound over the hook away from the body, while the ribbing is brought over the hook towards the body.

The hackle is wound in, and pulled down below the hook in the usual way. The colour is either dyed claret or natural red, according to taste. One of the unusual features of the

40

Mallard and Claret is that it is frequently dressed with a cock's hackle, even though it is a wet fly. This is probably to add to its working powers in still water where it reigns supreme.

The bed of silk is provided for the wings, and the slips are prepared. The danger to avoid is a splitting of the fibres, and there are two ways of removing these sections from the opposing feathers without disruption. One method is to mark out the fibres, then tear them away from the feather with a section of the quill adhering to them. This is quite simple for large wings, as in some salmon flies, but for small wings it is difficult. I prefer to mark out the sections gently with the point of the scissors, being careful not to pull the fibres away from their companions, as is the case with stronger feathers. Then I slide the blade under the tip of the section, move it down towards the roots, and snip it out.

The routine for winging is as outlined previously, except that special care must be exercised not to apply too much pressure. These rather frail feathers, like barred mallard and teal, do make a thin wing; some dressers like to reinforce them by using two slips from each wing, making four in all, which must be carefully matched. I must add that these soft wings are always in the downswept style for trout flies. It is therefore important to build up the bed of silk to a height equal to the hump of the hackle, and if the top centre fibres of the hackle are twitched out before they are divided, this hump is kept to a minimum.

You should have discovered that there is a theme running through this book: to demonstrate the processes of fly dressing, leaving the patterns of fly to introduce themselves as required by this purpose. The Mallard and Claret is one of a family prepared in the same fashion, including the Mallard and Green, Mallard and Red, Mallard and Gold and many others.

Tying a Peter Ross

Our next fly has the distinction of being unique. Though there is no fly quite like the Peter Ross, it will serve as an introduction to new techniques as well as to the family of flies having wings of barred teal, which is a repetition of the above group, Teal and Red, etc.

The Peter Ross is started in the same way as the Mallard and Claret, but in order to collect some new material, let us dress it on a large size of hook, say an 8. Now, instead of using the very fine gossamer thread, which would be wasteful, we use a slightly thicker grade called 'Naples'. The shade of silk need not match exactly the colour of the fly. In the Mallard and Claret, we may have used either claret or black, and black is sufficient for the Peter Ross. We run on the silk, tie in the tippets in the usual way, but next we have to tie in some fine oval tinsel, followed by flat tinsel, both silver. The flat tinsel is nipped in immediately to the right of the ribbing. It helps if a fine point is cut on to the end of this tinsel with scissors, then, having smoothed the rough edges between the finger-nails, two diagonal turns will help to maintain the tinsel at an angle for easy winding.

The silk is wound evenly back to a point half-way along the shank, care being taken to keep the tension and to make an even bed for the tinsel. The tinsel is wound to this same point, each turn butting up against the next with no overlapping, no unsightly gaps. This is then lashed down, the spare end being cut away, and the ragged edge smoothed with the finger-nail to prevent the thread from fraying on it. Immediately in front of the tinsel, a small portion of red seal's fur is dubbed in to conceal the untidy finish. The ribbing is spiralled up the body, over the dubbing, and tied off. If there is an untidy gap between the tinsel and the tail, a turn or two of the ribbing will cover it.

A black hen's hackle is next tied in, to the usual wet fly requirements, and finally a pair of teal wings, selected and put on as were the mallard. The fly is finished, and with it the stages of making a tinselled body have been mastered. I must also mention that many dressers tie in a fine tinsel at the end of the body, then run it down to the tail and back again. This is equally effective, and does combat the tendency to bulging at the tail where the tinsel crosses over the tying silk binding. One of the secrets in making a perfect Peter Ross lies in balancing the body correctly. The tinselled section should never exceed one half of the length of the shank, in order to leave room for the dubbing and hackle which follow it. Crowding the eye of the hook is one of the signs of bad fly dressing.

This fly is going to be a peg for me to hang up a new hat. Let us introduce some modern materials now. Modernization serves two purposes: firstly, it increases the attractiveness of the fly, and secondly, it makes the fly dresser's tasks more simple. In order to understand how these are applied to the Peter Ross, let us take a glance at its standard formula:

Tail – golden pheasant tippet.
Body – two-thirds flat silver tinsel, one-third red seal's fur.
Ribbing – fine silver oval tinsel.
Wings – barred teal.
Hackle – black hen.

Two ways of simplification strike the mind. The ribbing can be eliminated, and the seal's fur may be replaced by a more amenable material, such as wool. If you employ a fluorescent wool, this will increase the fly's appeal, especially in coloured water or conditions of poor or diffused light. The choice lies between the simple daylight fluorescent wools (D.F.M.) or the 'Depth Ray Fire', which is obtainable in floss, wool or chenille. The 'Depth Ray Fire' transmits light in the same way as 'shot silk'. The two different materials are equally effective, and, in my experience, add to the catch in the conditions that I have indicated.

My own way of using fluorescence in the Peter Ross is to tease out a small portion of the wool, then dub it in as if it were a body fur. It must be used sparingly, and not bound too tightly to the hook in order to have the effect of points of fire from the straggly fibres.

The main reason for ribbing over tinsel is to increase the flash of the body. We need to find a brighter substitute. Lurex, which is a plastic material, is the answer, for it is brighter than tinsel, though obtainable in the same colours, as well as in copper, scarlet, blue, orange, white and green. It can be bought in yard strips, or on spools of a width of one-thirty-second of an inch, which is most suitable for our purpose.

A length of this tough lurex replaces both the tinsel and the ribbing. It is wound up the body in the usual way, and ribbed tightly over the wool dubbing. The fly is hackled and winged in the usual way. The resulting fly has been simplified; at the same time, its brightness has been greatly enhanced.

At this juncture, we may consider the relative merits of silk and nylon as tying threads, for although the dealers normally supply silks only, many dressers have found that stocking repair thread is a suitable substitute, for it is finer, cheaper, and stronger than silk. Its one great drawback is that you can only buy it in shades to match the stockings; that is, black and various shades of brown. It is particularly useful for ultra-small flies, such as midges put up on 20 and 18 hooks. Having been seduced by nylon for a while, I have now reached a compromise, using the two threads selectively, according to the size of hook and shade of thread required. The constant use of silk does teach you the exact pressure to exert, just short of disaster. As speed comes, you also teach yourself to twitch away the spare ends without pausing to pick up scissors or razor-blade. Finally, the nylon does tend to unravel easily and catch up on tiny ridges of skin. In short, they both have their advantages, and you need both in your cabinet.

Materials

Here is a summary of the materials we need to add to our collection, assuming that the hooks have already been acquired.

Bronze mallard shoulder feathers.
Blue mallard secondaries (for the Butcher).
Light teal flank feathers.
Red fluorescent wool.
Golden pheasant tippets for tails.
Red ibis substitute (for Butcher tails).
Flat silver tinsel (fine).
Flat gold tinsel (fine).
Oval silver tinsel (fine).
Gold ditto.
Silver and gold lurex, on spools.
Black and claret naples tying silk.
Black 'Nylusta' stocking repair thread.

You might also care to experiment with a bottle of liquid wax. It helps the dubbing to stick to the thread, but is a bit messy, so keep a bottle of spirit handy, with a cloth for wiping the fingers after use.

You will also note that I have included two more materials, to bring the Butcher family within reach. These are dressed quite easily, using tinsel bodies and hackles from the collection.

Tinsels tarnish in time. They should be stored in airtight boxes in a dry place, and care should be taken to avoid handling them with damp fingers. When dull, they may be polished with a soft cloth, and even tarnish may be eradicated with a little jeweller's rouge.

9 How to Dress Mayflies

The Mayfly and its Life Cycle

Mayflies are treated separately, not because they are more difficult to dress than other flies, but because they, too, will introduce new materials, and new techniques. The artificial fly is fished in many styles, including the wet pattern and the nymph. It is not my purpose to discuss the ethics of using these last two, but I should mention in passing that on some waters they would be condemned, for they are very killing during the 'duffer's fortnight'. I leave them on one side, for the wet fly presents no dressing problems, and the nymphs are dealt with in the section devoted to the simple steps of constructing other nymphs and beetles. Here, we will concern ourselves with dry fly. Some reference must be made to entomology at this stage, for the fly dresser is concerned with copying the natural fly at all stages of its adult life, from the moment that it breaks free from its nymphal shuck to the time when the dead body of the fly is swept away downstream as a spent gnat. It is not often realized that not only will trout become preoccupied with a certain fly, but will sometimes feed exclusively on it at a certain stage of its development. In no other fly is this so clearly marked as in the Mayfly, when the angler can see the large insects from afar, and determine the duns from the spinners.

What are duns and spinners? The Mayfly belongs to an order of flies known as the *Ephemeroptera*, which is distinguished by passing through two adult stages. From the first winged stage, when the fly is somewhat drab in colour and heavy on the wing, the fly passes to its final stage by bursting from the skin of the dull sub-imago, as the scientist calls this unusual first stage. A bright, gaily coloured insect emerges, being lighter on the wing, with a stronger flight. These two stages are known to angler and fly dresser as the 'dun' and the 'spinner'. A further complication lies in the difference in coloration between the males and females. This is rarely a factor in the dun stages, but many spinners are completely different, and the trout know it. On the whole, male spinners of these flies are not so important,

45

for it is the female that must return to the water to lay her eggs, and, when this task is finished, she dies, to be swept away by the current, with her limp wings spread out on the water – an easy target for the waiting fish.

To relate this to the Mayfly is not difficult. The fisherman calls the duns 'Green Drakes'. The colour is the fact behind this name, but, as in all these flies, there is variation from river to river. Some waters produce a yellow race, which results in the 'Yellow Drake'. The female spinner takes its name from its light gauzy wings – it is baptized the 'Grey Drake' – while the male spinner, which so rarely tumbles into the water, is the 'Black Drake'. Finally, the dead female on the stream is the 'Spent Gnat'. You will guess from this that there is a profusion of copies of Mayflies. There is – they probably exceed a hundred! Again, it makes sense to rely on a limited number of patterns to begin with, expanding the supply of materials gradually to include others. After all, the Mayfly season barely lasts a fortnight. I do not wish to digress into the question of tactics, but the Mayfly, being a comparatively hefty artificial, is a tricky missile to deliver accurately. Initially, we might well concentrate on the hackled flies, as the bulky wings do find any breath of air that is moving between the banks.

Materials for the Mayfly

There are special hooks for Mayflies, being longer in the shank, just as the natural fly is longer than most of his cousins. For dry fly fishing, the lighter wire hooks with up-turned eyes are suitable, size 10 approximating to the average size.

Many of the hackles for Mayflies are exotic and costly. Here are some of the names; mandarin duck, French partridge, Rouen drake, summer duck, and Egyptian goose. I content myself with an equally effective but less expensive feather from the flank of the mallard. These are perfect, either in their natural grey or dyed yellow or green, but because they are soft they have to be supported by a hackle or two from a cockerel, dyed to match.

For the moment, we may select a single material for the bodies of all of the Mayfly patterns; a piece of delicately-tinted plastic sheeting, or alternatively a hank of natural raffia will supply our needs economically. Let us fashion a Green Drake: better still, let us make half a dozen, for anglers usually need a quantity of a firm favourite, and it is easier to work with materials laid out in advance than to keep hunting through the cabinet for fresh materials every few minutes.

Tying a Mayfly

The first hook is placed in the vice, the silk wound on to the bend, and the tail fibres tied in. These should be three strands of a cock-pheasant's centre-tail feather, one of the most important of materials which we had collected pre-

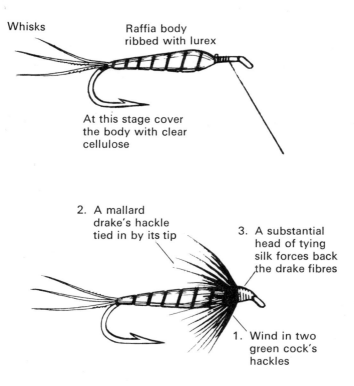

Fig. 11. Stages in tying a mayfly

47

viously. The ideal is to arrange two of these tail-whisks to form a wide V, with the third one in the centre, as in the natural fly. The thin strip of raffia is nipped under the shank, and also a thin strip of silver lurex for the ribbing. The thread is taken back to the shoulder of the fly, and the body formed. The aim is to shape the body like a carrot, the thick end lying to the head. The lurex is ribbed over the raffia body, tied down, and the spare ends of material snipped away.

At this stage, put in two whip-turns to hold the body secure. Then remove the hook from the vice, and cover the body with a layer of clear cellulose varnish to give the fly an appearance of translucency. It can be hung up to dry on a length of fishing-line suspended between two points. Thus the bodies of all of the flies are finished in an assembly line production, for when the last is completed, the first will be crying out for its legs and wings!

Returning to the first fly, two green cock's hackles are wound in, followed by the mallard flank feather. There is a special colour called 'green drake', which is a drab, deep shade. The mallard hackle is tied in by the tip, first having had its fluffy base fibres stripped away. The main part of the feather is pulled out at right angles to the stalk, which isolates the tip for tying in, and makes these clinging feathers start out from the hook on winding. It may be necessary to strip the fibres from one whole side of the stalk if the feather is rather thick and coarse. Some dressers always do this, others do not.

Finally, it is necessary to build up a substantial head of tying silk to force the drake fibres back slightly to give an effect of gauzy wings. The yellow drake, which is a colour variation for some waters, is simply made by using hackles of that colour. My own grey drake effect is achieved by using white or badger cock hackles behind the natural grey mallard flank feathers.

The Fanwing Mayfly

If you want to make a fly that shows off the fly dresser's art to the layman, the fanwing Mayfly is the answer. The name is self-descriptive. The wings are a pair of matching drake flank feathers in the same colours as before, but they are stronger and smaller. When the soft fibres are stripped away, the two feathers are placed back to back, and bound down on to the top of the hook in the usual way. They are

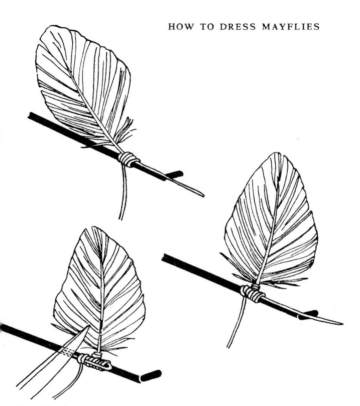

Fig. 12. Putting on fanwings

raised upright and several turns of silk made around the stalks at the base. The spare ends of stalk are pulled to the rear and tied to the hook-shank, the surplus being cut away. This keeps the wings firmly in position. A cock hackle is wound in front of the wings, another behind, and the fly is finished.

We must now tackle the problem of making a spent May-fly, which is characterized by its outspread wings and sparse hackle, for the artificial must settle into the surface film, being supported by these wings, and not by the legs. To enhance the impression of mortality, the colours are 'washed out' into sombre whites and blacks.

The body of the fly is formed in the same way. Then the wings are prepared. These are hackle points from a black cock. If most of the body fibres are removed from either side of the stalk, a small diamond of feather is left at

49

the tip. Four of these are tied on top of the hook-shank with figure-of-eight turns, two on either side, so that they lie flat. My method of doing this is to put a drop of the clear varnish on top of the hook in the desired position, and allow it to grow tacky. This holds the hackle points while they are bound on. One side of the fly should be completed at a time, it being a matter of taste whether the two wings are tied separately or together. As with the fanwings, the hackle stalks should be whipped down for a short length, and a forwards or rearwards sweep can be given to the wings by pulling them backwards or forwards before tying. The surplus ends are snipped away.

The hackle should be sparse, as in all spent flies. In this case, it may be either a white or badger cock's feather. Two turns in front of the points, and two behind, are ample. This is a suitable juncture to indicate that all female spinners have their 'spent gnat' stage. The Pheasant Tail is one fine example, though with these shorter hooks, it is customary only to tie in one pair of hackle points. During the process of dressing a wide range of patterns, many hackles will be used. By carefully refraining from winding on the feathers up to the hilt, the points can be saved, and placed in a box for the purpose, for it is wasteful to throw away three to five hackles on a fly, when they are in such short supply.

Other Methods and Materials

Let us now introduce some other methods and materials for the Mayfly.

One invention allows fly dressers to employ the normal size of hooks. This is the detached body. With a little ingenuity, these bodies can be made of such things as nylon, bristle, rubber solution. cork, and so on. The most convenient way to obtain detached bodies for Mayflies is to buy them from the dealer. Veniard now stocks a most impressive hollow plastic body, resembling somewhat a length of valve rubber, though tapered and sealed at one end. They can be purchased in a wide range of colour, cream, light green-olive, light brown-olive, etc. If the thread closes the open end of the tube in preparing the fly, an airtight buoyancy tank is built into the artificial, keeping it afloat permanently. Furthermore, the bodies have segments made in the moulding process. To add the tails, it is only necessary to pierce the sealed end with a pin, push the three fibres through, and reseal with cellulose varnish. After the body has been lashed down to the hook-shank, the wings and legs are made in the usual way.

Another way of providing the wings with a gauzy effect of light filtration is by using a hackle. We saw how hackle fibres could be divided and pulled below the hook when we were making the winged wet fly. Similarly, these fibres can be manipulated into any other direction, and if a hackle of another colour is wound round the 'shaped' one, startling effects can be gained.

For instance, to relate this to our spent spinner, a long-fibred black cock's hackle is wound on, thoroughly moistened, then divided into equal portions on each side of the hook in the 'spent' position. A few figure-of-eight windings will hold them there, and a white hackle makes an aura round them.

For ordinary duns and spinners, these two groups of fibres could be held upright for the split-wing dry fly, or swept over the eye of the hook for the 'shaving-brush' style, which is simply an advanced-wing fly, using hackle fibres instead of the more solid slips of feather.

The permutations of Mayfly patterns are endless, but they rarely introduce new processes of fly dressing. It boils down to a simple, expensive process of collecting exotic materials; but such is their beauty, I cannot resist this temptation. The flies, too, become collectors' items, and mine are usually given to friends who do not fish with them. My wife often sews one to her blouse! For the moment however, let us restrict ourselves to gathering the items we need for practical needs outlined above, and then your bankruptcy will not be on my conscience. As for that letter you are writing to the land of the Pharaohs, I do not know the Arabic for Egyptian Goose.

Natural raffia.
Cock hackles, dyed yellow and green drake.
Grey drake (mallard) flank feathers, natural grey and dyed yellow and green drake.
Grey drake, small round breast feathers for fanwings, natural, and dyed green and yellow drake.
Long-shanked Mayfly hooks, upturned eye, sizes 10 and 12.
Hollow plastic Mayfly bodies, light green-olive.

10 Nymphs and Beetles

These are easy flies to dress. In fact, many of them consist of little more than the bodies of artificial flies that are already familiar, minus the wings, and in some cases, the hackles, too. For this reason, it is a good opportunity to take stock. You are probably still suffering from some minor vexations? Perhaps I can salve some of these hurts with some tips from my own experience. Like every craft, fly dressing has some basic techniques which are so simple that they are overlooked, and for this reason, I make no apology for reminding you of them.

What Do You Think of it So Far?

It is most important to work with clean fingers. White wings, hackles and silks do not impress friends if they have been turned to grey. Make it a rule always to wash your hands before sitting down to the bench. If you work with your hands during the day, you will undoubtedly have many ridges of skin on your fingers as a result of small cuts and abrasions. You will not be aware of this until the tying thread keeps catching up on them. As farmers rank among the best fly dressers, these marks of honest labour will not interfere with the fly if a softening cream is worked into the skin after washing.

As in painting, half the battle for a good fly lies in preparation, which also removes the frustration of leaving the bench at a crucial stage to hunt through packets and boxes. Lay out the materials that you know you will need, after referring to the book of listed dressings.

The thread keeps breaking? This irritating habit of snapping the thread is common to beginners who apply too much pressure. It disappears with practice, when you know that too much pressure can destroy the set of a pair of wings. Alternatively, try nylon or 'Naples' thread.

You may have difficulty with positioning the hackle for a winged wet fly. To avoid an unpleasant hump on top of the shank, and to make the division of the fibres easy, snip out the centre fibres on top of the hook-shank. Most wet flies have far too much hackle. To help you to grasp the fibres to pull them below the hook, choose a long-fibred hackle, for you can snip the surplus length away to suit your taste, after the fly has been finished.

I expect that the wings are your main problem. If the fibres fly apart, before you tie them in, stroke them with the dubbing-needle coated in thin varnish, and give them another touch at the tips when the fly is complete. It is a good plan to keep your varnish in different strengths, and one small bottle of a diluted solution is invaluable for treating wings and limp hackles. Mix the varnish with the thinners obtainable for a modest sum from the dealer. Some dressers also put a drop of varnish on the place where the wings are to be fixed.

There is rarely any need to hurry when making a few flies for your own box, but you may be feeling the urge to sharpen up your technique. Of course, the processes can be speeded up by using the fingers more instead of picking up tools. For example, the longer hackles may be wound in by the fingers, and I seldom employ the larger sizes of hackle pliers. Furthermore, spare ends of silk, hackle, herl and wire can be twitched out rather than cut. The technique is simple. After a turn of the tying silk has bound down the material, the remnant is gripped firmly and tweaked sharply against this silk, which must be kept very tight by the other hand. It results in a very neat finish, flush to the hook. The secret lies in the tight thread acting as a guillotine, but the action must be bold. A half-hearted tug will probably pull the fly to pieces. Practise this.

On the other hand, you may experience those days when nothing goes right. The reasons for this are inexplicable, but it does not mean that you are a rotten fly dresser, for even experts suffer likewise. One thing to avoid is sitting down to work immediately after finishing some form of vigorous activity, for this seems to cause a slight tremor to the fingers, which ruins the fly. It is far better to sit down calmly for half an hour, and come to the bench thoroughly relaxed.

Nymphs and Beetles

Now, our half-time is over. We must turn our hand to the making of nymphs and beetles.

Many of these patterns were introduced by that master of fly fishing, G. E. M. Skues. More recently, Frank Sawyer has invented some patterns for the stream fisher, while Tom

Ivens has done the same thing for the reservoir angler. From a structural viewpoint, the nymph resembles the adult fly which it will become, except that the wings are contained in wing-cases, which are represented by a hump at the shoulder of the fly, while the gills and other appendages, are copied by a hackle, usually clipped short. In many cases, this is omitted altogether.

The first duty of the artificial is to dive cleanly through the surface film. This is achieved by weighting the body. Lead wire can be used, but generally this gives the nymph so much weight that it plummets straight to the bottom. The choice lies between a wire undervest, or the use of a fine wire in place of the tying thread. I pin my faith on the first alternative, using 5-amp. fuse-wire, for I find that the fine copper wire recommended by Frank Sawyer, will cut through the frail herls. Let us put this into effect on a Pheasant Tail nymph.

Tying a Pheasant Tail Nymph

The hook, size 12, is fixed in the vice, and a length of thread wound on in the usual way. Next, two tail whisks are attached. These are taken from the centre feathers of a cock pheasant's tail. The ribbing of fine oval gold tinsel is nipped under the hook, followed by the herls for the body.

Fig. 13. Pheasant Tail Nymph

These are also herls from the same feather as the whisks, but you should select fibres with a glowing ruddy colour. Inferior tail feathers are dullish and the black markings too obtrusive. Having done this, bring the silk up the body a short distance, and tie in the fuse-wire, which, when wound in, will help taper the body, making it thicker towards the head. Now, wind the silk towards the head, stopping about a third of the way short of the eye, to leave room for the thorax and wing-cases. Wind on the fuse-wire vest, followed by the herls, being careful to thicken the body as described. Follow this with the ribbing, which can be spiralled in the opposite direction to the herls to prevent it from burying between the turns, a danger with all-narrow ribbings.

The best part of the herls will have been used up, so these may be removed with the spare end of wire. A further six herls are now tied in on top of the hook, for these will form the wing-cases. Most Pheasant Tail nymphs have a thorax made from the herls themselves, but I prefer to show a change of colour, usually darker, for nymph thoraces; thus we dub in a portion of mole's fur, wind on a small hump, and bring the fibres over the top to indicate the wing-cases. The six fibres are then divided on top of the hook, three on each side, and kept into the horizontal plane with figure-of-eight turns. They are then clipped short to the shank, say one-tenth of an inch, and the fly finished off in the usual way.

Tying a Corixa

The significant differences in beetle dressings are that the whole bodies are plumper, dubbings of seal's fur being a good medium, and the wing-cases go the length of the body, from tail to head. It is a customary precaution to tie

Fig. 14. Corixa

in a matching hen's hackle in the wet fly position to simulate the legs. For the wing-cases, a stouter feather is preferred, woodcock or waterhen primaries being a sensible choice. Blacks, browns, and dark greens are logical colours to employ, and a wide silver ribbing gives the effect of the air-bubbles that beetles collect from the surface.

In recent years, one of the water-bugs has emerged as a factor in the diet of trout in still water. It also brings out the fly dressing processes. This fly, both natural and artificial, is the Corixa, or Water-boatman.

Having made the underbody, and tied in a length of white

floss silk for the body, stout brown thread and oval silver tinsel for the ribbings, and a strip of dark feather for the wing-cases, a plump body is made. The ribbings cross each other by being wound in opposite directions, and the wing-cases are brought over the body, then tied down. A ginger hackle, stiff in fibre, is given two turns only, before being divided on either side of the hook, and maintained there by figure-of-eight turns. These two groups of fibres copy the paddles of the Boatman. Finally, a buff or white hen's hackle is tied in, and fixed in the wet fly position for the legs.

One word of warning I must interpose. Should you consult a treatise on entomology, you will find the various appendages to these creatures described in quite scientific terms. Remember that we are only concerned to recognize the structure of the fly in simple words. Legs may not be legs at all, but the fly dresser knows where the hackle has to go.

I have pointed out that this book is concerned with the operations of fly dressing, and that patterns are only introduced to demonstrate these processes and the materials involved. I should pay tribute to the series of flies invented by Tom Ivens for reservoir fishing, for they are simple to fashion, and the materials are easily found. I shall include some of these materials in the list, and an appendix to the book shows sources for obtaining dressing prescriptions.

And now to add to our collection, for the bodies of nymphs and beetles:

Ostrich herl, green, brown and black.
Seal's fur, pale olive, amber.
Floss silk, white.
Swan's herl, green, yellow.
Brown thread for ribbing.
5-amp. fuse-wire.
Black, white and red horsehair.

11 The Use of Hair

Hair as a Tying Medium

We have seen previously that the wings of flies are of three or four basic colours, grey, brown, white, and red. These could be taken from a simple range of feathers, such as from the wings of poultry and starling. The same is true of hair when it is used in the place of feather for the wings of flies, for although many exotic fibres are imported from abroad, the first needs may be served by two tails, one from the red squirrel, one from the grey. It adds to the fascination of fly dressing to collect the fur of polar bears or monkeys. However, a careful look at the two squirrel tails I have mentioned reveals a great variety of colour, such as pure white and black, brown and grey, and miscellaneous barred fibres equivalent to teal and mallard wings.

Let us discover how to use the hair before we discuss the fibres we may collect. Hair is used mainly for the wings of wet flies, especially streamers, though it does make an appearance on certain dry flies. On occasion the hair can be used in the place of a hackle, particularly on large patterns.

In all these cases, the bodies and tails of the flies are formed in the customary fashion, except that it should be remembered that as hair takes up more room than feather, slightly more space must be allowed for it between the end of the body and the eye of the hook. One of my favourite lake flies is a hair-wing Mallard and Claret. The body and hackle are put on in the usual way, and then a barred section is cut from the tail of a brown squirrel's tail. This is easily performed if the selected fibres are twisted together while the scissors are run down to their roots.

One of the commonest faults is to try to remove too broad a section of hair. Bearing in mind that these hairs will splay out when tied in, a narrow band should be taken. If the bunch of hair is gripped between the fingers of the left hand, it will be noticed that there are many soft, fluffy fibres at the base, which should be combed out. Before tying in, a drop of cellulose varnish should be applied to the top of the hook, and another at the base of the wing section. My own method of tying in the hair is to hold it at an angle to the

Fig. 15. Putting on a hair wing, with a locking turn

hook-shank, take a turn of thread round it, and while this is being tightened, I roll the wing into position on top of the hook. I now make about three turns round the hair and the hook, before raising the wing section and making a complete turn around the hair alone. This makes a slight bump which is covered up by subsequent turns of silk, moving towards the tail of the fly. The roots of the hair are cut away at an angle to make a step. Then, when the silk is wound back in even turns to the eye, a neatly-tapered head should result.

It will be found that hair is an easily managed material, but as it is quite slippery, varnish should be applied generously. Finally, the wing can be trimmed to a suitable length.

I find that hair is too heavy to make a good floating fly, but it is used in some of the sedges. The palmer hackle is left out, and after the hair wing has been formed, the shoulder hackle is wound in to cover up the roots. It is possible to divide the wing into two sections by figure-of-eight bindings.

How to Dye Hair, Fur and Feather

The tremendous advantage of hair is that it enables the amateur dresser to construct most effective salmon flies without collecting a host of quite expensive feathers, or mastering the relatively difficult processes of marrying fibres for the underwings. Sections of hair dyed in various colours, replace these feather sections, and are simply tied in the desired positions, colour by colour. Being a heavy fly, often used in faster waters, the hair for these salmon hairwings must be stouter, and Bucktail is the best choice. Since a pattern like the Jock Scott, one among many similar flies, will need hair in scarlet, blue and yellow, the home fly dresser should be able to dye his own materials. It goes without saying that hackles, herls, and furs can be dyed for flies, large or small.

In the old days of Halford, dyeing was a messy business, and they revelled in it. Nowadays it is quite simple. Apart from the packets of dye, which are cheap, you will need two containers, one perforated one which fits inside the other.

According to the colour, about half a teaspoonful of dye powder is added to a teacup of boiling water. The mixture is brought to the boil, then allowed to cool a little before the material is immersed. When this material has taken up enough of the colour, it is fixed by the addition of a tablespoonful of vinegar (or acetic acid). Then the material is removed, rinsed thoroughly in cold water, and dried out. My method of drying is to press the material between sheets of newspaper, and put it into the airing cupboard.

Correct dyeing comes with experience, and unless you are lucky, the first efforts will be disappointing. It is hard to allow for the drying making the colour slightly lighter. Indeed, dark shades should be left in the solution until it is cold before fixing. The answer is to begin with straightforward colours, orange, red, blue, and so on, and aim at the delicate shades of light olive, when you have a trained eye.

One or two of the old dyes still hold our affections, and picric acid, in particular, makes a first-class shade of yellow drake. But the days of weak tea and onion juice have gone for ever, thank goodness.

Hair and fur can be dyed directly, though many feel it is a sensible precaution to wash it first. Feathers will not take up a dye until they have been soaked in a solution of soap or detergent to counteract the effect of the natural oils. It is this degreasing that makes the natural hackle score over the artificially tinted one. The feathers should be washed clean of the soap solution before being immersed in the dye.

One last precaution. It is easier to make a colour stronger

by adding more dye before fixing, but be careful to remove the material first, for the powder will cause an unpleasant effect of measles if it comes into contact with it.

It would be pointless to list here all the dye colours in the catalogue. Suffice to say that you will find the shade you need in the forty stocked by Veniard, and if you are still in difficulty, you may obtain a colour chart to select from. You may also buy cheaply any of the eight fluorescent colours.

The Choice of Hair

The development of hairwing flies is a boon for the amateur dresser. The flies are efficient, the material easy to manage, and for the most part, cheap to buy. I will now describe some of the particular hairs obtainable, and the winged flies for which they can be used.

For the relatively small group of dry flies, the brown and grey squirrel tails will serve most needs. It is obvious that only the sedge-type flies can be imitated, for hair is heavier than feather, and will cause a fly to ride upside down if dressed in the upright position.

Bucktail comes in natural brown and white, and should also be dyed, blue, red, yellow and green. For the smaller sizes of hairwing, I prefer goat's hair, which is fine, though wiry, and does not take up too much room on the shank. For teal-winged flies, such as the Peter Ross, some barred fibres may be found on the grey squirrel's tail, while the brown squirrel will do the same service for barred mallard. Perfectionists may take this a stage farther by using silver baboon for the Peter Ross, for this hair has a more exact black and white striping. In fact, if you should wish to extend your collection of hair beyond the basic essentials I have outlined, Tom Saville of Nottingham specializes in any pelt ranging from polar bear to silver baboon. For the moment, let us content ourselves with practical considerations.

Natural brown and white bucktail.
Dyes in the following colours: red, yellow, blue, green, orange, claret, and black.
Grey squirrel tail.
Brown squirrel tail.
Stoat's tail.
Goat's hair for dyeing.
Long-shanked hooks for streamer flies.

A selection of long hackles for streamer flies, in red, blue, yellow, etc. These hackles are simply tied in back to back on the top of the hook to form the wings.

12 Making Tube Flies

The Advantages of Tube Flies

Occasionally there is a complete breakthrough in a sphere of angling, and the invention of the tube fly must rank as a fine example. Consider the old-fashioned salmon hook with its long point and huge barb. The chances of setting such an iron in a heavy current with a long line were never certain. If it were possible to substitute a small treble hook, how much easier it would be! The tube fly combines the virtues of the spinning lure with the traditional artificial fly, for the signal fault of a Devon minnow is that it is so heavy that it cannot be made to flutter slowly in the current. But these are angling facts, and are slightly outside my province. I wish to show you that I am really sold on the tube flies, for easy hooking, quick changing, and efficient working in the water.

What are the advantages from the viewpoint of the fly dresser? There are many. Firstly, the tube is easy to adorn with fur and feather. Secondly, the standard salmon and sea trout patterns can all be copied on tubes. Since the trickier winging processes are not needed, the tube is quicker to make. The absence of the wings means that simple range of materials will meet all your needs, and bearing in mind that many plumages for salmon flies are both expensive and hard to obtain, the tube fly is cheaper, as a quick glance at any tackle catalogue will reveal. It is the fly of the future, but besides being strictly practical, it can be pleasing to the eye, even though it is not the work of art of a fully robed salmon fly in all its glory.

Types of Tubes

The down-to-earth amateur might prefer to start from scratch by finding his own polythene tubing of a conveniently narrow diameter, cutting it into lengths to suit his own fishing. I have seen some excellent tube flies constructed from the tubes of ball-point pens, which, when empty, have been cleaned of every trace of ink. The brass nozzles of these pens have had the ball knocked out, leaving a hole for the line, and when fitted into the end of the finished fly, they provide the nose cone for deep fishing. For myself, I do not care for the tube flies with obtrusive brass heads, preferring all the weight to be in the tube casing itself. From the point of view of convenience, I rely on the 'Slipstream' series of tubes, for which Veniards are the U.K. agents. These are available in a handy range of weights and lengths.

There are four types of these tubes. Type 'A' is a straight-forward polythene tube with moulded ends to prevent the dressing from slipping off. This is the lightest of the tubes, and in the half-inch length is suitable for trout flies. I use these extensively for reservoir trouting with greased line. Type 'B' is a stronger, heavier tube, the end of which is sleeved to hold the hook-eye, and maintain its alignment. Type 'C' is jacketed with aluminium, and thus makes for an ideal middle-water fly on still water, or a heavier one for fast currents. Lastly, type 'D' is plastic-lined brass; an exceptionally heavy tube for big waters in the spring or the deep sunk lure on lakes. The sizes of all of these tubes vary from half-an-inch to two inches.

Since the tube fly is slipped on to the cast, then run down on to a treble hook, a brief note is appropriate about which size hook to use with a certain length of tube. From half an inch up to an inch, I use a 16 treble, from 1 inch to 1½ inches a No. 14, and for longer tubes than this I employ a No. 12. By confining myself to these three sizes of hook, I can become a quick change artist on the river bank.

Tying Techniques

The very first problem of making a tube fly is how to keep the tube rigid while tying the materials to it. My own method is to keep near by a selection of darning needles which fit

Fig. 16. Tube fitted on to a needle

into the tube. The needle must be tapered steeply enough for the tube to be jammed tight. The right size of needle is jammed firmly between the jaws of the vice, and the tube is slid on to it. The perfect situation is when the tube is held securely when it butts up against the vice. It is obvious that in order to turn the tube on the needle, it is only necessary to slip it off the taper slightly. I find that the diameters of these tubes are consistent, and after one or two raids on the work basket, I have been able to put aside three needles that hold all the tubes I dress. At first, though, you may have to test dozens of needles before you find good ones, so treasure them!

You remember that we collected the tail of a stoat when we were investigating hair-winged flies? Let us put it to work on one of the most simple, yet killing patterns, the Stoat Tail. The beauty of tube flies is that no one has yet frozen the dressings into standard formulae; there is no tradition, and the field is yours. In this fly, you may choose any body colour you like. My own preference is for black floss silk, with a ribbing of narrow silver lurex.

The first step is to run on the tying silk, but here we notice one essential difference between tubes and hooks. Tubes use far more materials; indeed, in order to wind the silk evenly, you may need more than a yard of 'gossamer' silk. Although I like to wind evenly when using a tinsel body, for floss silks and dubbings, I run the thread to the bottom of the tube in wide spirals, having made the first few turns at the head to secure the spare end of the silk. Next, I tie in my ribbing, followed by the black floss. On tubes, I prefer the ribbing to go in to the left of the body-silk to prevent an ugly bulge at the end of the tube. Then the thread is returned towards the head of the fly, but enough room must be left for the hair wings. If you think of your orthodox hair-wings on a hook-shank, you will know the right distance, but something more than one-tenth of an inch is about right.

The floss silk body is made, spreading the silk to make a smooth layer instead of lumpy coils. This is followed by the ribbing, making the turns fairly wide. The spare ends are removed after they have been lashed down. Now the bare section of tube must be covered by an even layer of tying silk to form a bed for the wings. The secret of making a perfect tube fly lies in control of the thread. Each turn must be made to perform a task, and it must also be butted against its neighbour. Uneven winding, crossed turns, lead to a large, clumsy head and insecure wings.

These wings are made from sections of the hair from the

dark part of a stoat's tail. Each section is removed as described previously, and it is important to comb out any soft, short, fluffy fibres from the roots, after cutting out the tuft. The thread starts from the end of the body. The first portion of hair is held in place on the top of the tube, and trapped by the thread. The hair will spread out slightly around the tube, but it is vital to keep each section of hair to a minimum width when cutting it from the tail. A small pinch of fibres will be ample. There is also a tendency for the hair to twist, and it should be kept in alignment with the tube.

Now, if the tube is loosened gently on the needle, by giving it a slight turn towards the dresser, the next section of tube presents itself for treatment. Note that if the tube were turned in the opposite direction, you would be unwinding your fly, and the hair you have just put on will fall

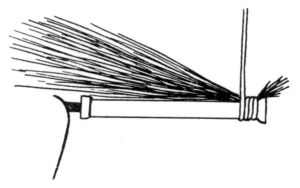

Fig. 17. Putting a hair wing on to a tube

off. The next section of hair is tied on, the fingers gently working it over the tube so that it mates up with the first section, leaving no unsightly gap between. The process is repeated until the wing is complete right round the tube. I can accomplish this in three sections, four at the most.

At this stage, I secure the hair with a few whip turns, and remove the tube from the needle in order to trim away the roots from the end of the tube. Then, when the tube has been replaced, the head is completed, whip-finished, and varnished. When you are skilled at forming your wings, you should be able to remove the roots from each section of hair after it is tied in, thus reducing the size of the head even more. I like to finish off with a coat or two of clear varnish, followed by black. Incidentally, even though black varnish appears to dry in an hour or two, leave it for twenty-four hours to become rock-hard. Always allow each coat of varnish to dry completely before adding the next. The first coat of the varnish will do little more than soak into the silk, and underseal it for the next.

So much for the simple tube fly made from a single body and wing. There are some tube fly patterns, like the Black Sambo, which do not even require the body to be dressed, but rely on the bare tube, veiled by hair. On the other hand, other patterns are more sophisticated, and are adorned with hackles as well as wings. Now, it is obvious that if the long, dark hair were superimposed on the short, light hackle, the latter would be entirely obscured. So we do the sensible thing, and we put the hackle over the wing, tying it in last.

Tying a Silver Blue

As I have remarked, you may study a traditional salmon fly, and convert it to a tube fly in your imagination. Let us pick an easy one, the Silver Blue. The low water pattern has a silver body, blue hackle and teal wing. We make the body of silver tinsel or lurex, ribbed with a fine oval silver tinsel, and we make the hair-wing from the grey squirrel's tail, in the usual way, but instead of tying off, the silk thread is returned to the point where the first piece of hair was tied in. This is the place for the hackle. We have the silver in the body, and the grey wing is equal to the teal wing. We must now introduce the blue. This can be either a blue cock or hen hackle, but I like dyed guinea fowl for tube flies, as it is somewhat bolder in appearance. Since the feather is thick, it must be stripped on one side, and tied in by the tip. Looking at the front of the feather, the left-hand fibres are the ones to be removed, for otherwise they would be crushed by the stalk. The hackle is given two good turns, and tied off. The fibres are then held to the rear while a turn of silk over their base will keep them pointing to the rear. The head is then completed, and the fly finished off in the way previously described.

There is no reason why a hackle should not be wound on a tube palmer-fashion, as in the Thunder and Lightning, while the trebles can be given a wisp of silk or hackle to match the main colour of the tube. In fact, to show how you can convert any standard salmon fly to its tube fly equivalent, I will make the comparison with two well-known patterns. At this stage, it is not necessary to unravel the mysteries of winging the salmon flies, for we shall discuss these in later chapters.

Two Popular Salmon Flies

Firstly, here is that popular favourite, the Thunder and Lightning.

Standard Dressing	*Tube Dressing*
Tag – Round silver tinsel and yellow floss.	None.
Tail – Golden pheasant crest and Indian crow.	None.
Butt – Black ostrich herl	None.
Body – Black floss.	Ditto.
Rib – Oval gold tinsel.	Gold lurex.
Hackle – Hot orange cock along the whole body.	Ditto.
Hackle (Throat) – Blue guinea fowl.	Ditto.
Wings – Strips of brown mallard.	Brown bucktail.
Sides – Jungle cock.	None.
Topping – Golden pheasant crest.	None.

It is immediately obvious that tremendous simplification has taken place in the tube fly. Not only are five items left out, but the tying in of wing slips and toppings are also absent. In fact, the tube fly takes a fraction of the time to dress, even compared with this simple strip-wing salmon fly. Now compare it with one of those beautiful mixed-wing flies, the Silver Doctor.

Standard Dressing	*Tube Dressing*
Tag – Round silver tinsel and yellow floss.	None.
Tail – Golden pheasant crest and blue chatterer.	None.
Butt – Scarlet wool.	None.
Body – Flat silver tinsel.	Ditto.
Rib – Oval silver tinsel.	Ditto.
Hackles (Throat) – A pale blue hackle followed by widgeon.	Natural guinea fowl. (Optional)

Wings – Mixed tippet in strands with strips of golden pheasant over, married strands of scarlet, blue and yellow swan, florican, bustard, peacock wing and light mottled turkey tail. Married narrow strips of teal and barred summer duck over, a topping over all.	Alternating strips of grey squirrel tail, and red, blue and yellow hair.
Head – Scarlet wool. Red varnish.	Red varnish.

The simplification is even greater, for the time-consuming construction of married wing-fibres is eliminated. It is no more difficult to make a hair-wing from strips of hair of different colours than it is to use a single colour. Of course, you must take care to keep these strips to reasonable widths, and to see that they do not slip out of position, but these easy precautions will not tax your patience unduly. Besides, whereas many salmon fly feathers are rare and costly, the hair, natural and dyed, is both cheap and plentiful. In the case of the Silver Doctor, for example, the best choice of hair to dye is that of the grey squirrel, identical to the 'natural' part of the wing. What could be more simple?

If you wish to adorn your tube flies, you may do so. Tags and butts are easily tied in, and a red wool butt might have been added to our Silver Doctor. Equally, the jungle cock cheeks could have been added, but generally, the tube fly has sprung out of the modern angler's practical needs, and not from the traditions of the past.

It is simple for a fly dresser to convert a local favourite salmon pattern to its tube equivalent, for from our two examples you will have learned that the two main colours of body and wing are very similar, and the selfsame hackle is tied over before the tube is completed. It may be that tube fly dressings will be codified as time goes by. At this moment, we may see that it is not necessary.

There is one last advantage to the tube. Bodies and heads may be dressed in separate sections, which increases both the size and range of the tubes. For example, a number of plain, tinselled bodies can be dressed to add to the tail of a tube when conditions require. And, finally, never neglect the trout-sized tube fly. I successfully use tubes dressed as Invicta, Peter Ross and Mallard and Claret, for the bodies may be dubbed with seal's fur or wool as in the normal hook fly.

Now, let us add to our collection.

Lightweight plastic tubes for sub-surface fishing in various lengths from $\frac{1}{2}$ in. to $1\frac{1}{2}$ in.

Medium-weight tubes, jacketed with aluminium for mid-water or faster currents, to the same lengths and with a few of 2 in. Heavy brass tubes in the larger sizes for deep water or very heavy streams, 1 in. and 2 in.

Treble hooks to match these tubes.

A selection of darning needles to fit the holes.

Guinea fowl hackles, natural grey and dyed blue.

13 Dressing Low Water Flies

Flies for a Purpose

I am using these patterns as a bridge between the simple trout fly and the fully dressed salmon fly in all its glory. Low water salmon flies resemble trout flies in many ways, and hold many processes of tying in common with sea trout patterns. At the same time, they will help us to acquaint ourselves with methods and materials peculiar to their big sisters. It is better to approach salmon flies by way of the low water fly for this reason. It is also a practical step, for the majority of us are holiday anglers. We go to a remote corner of the country, in Scotland, Ireland, Wales, or the Western Counties in the summer. Salmon are there, but the days are bright, the water is warm, and the level of the rivers has fallen. The low-water flies were designed to catch fish under these conditions when used in conjunction with the greased line method of fishing, still so-called in spite of the fact that modern plastic floating lines perform well without greasing. The fly is lightly dressed so that it rides just beneath the surface of the water.

As in tube flies, there is hardly a list of the standard dressings, for if a popular Spring pattern were to be converted to low water needs, many of the feathers would have to be left out. There is no reason why any fully dressed fly should not be adapted; you will again have to employ your imagination to supply the answers. Nevertheless, there are a handful of accepted favourites, and who has not heard tell of the Blue Charm?

The basic fact of salmon flies is that they are big. The hooks for standard patterns are known as 'Ordinary Forged'. They have a black japanned appearance with an upturned eye. The range in sizes goes from about half-an-inch to five times that length, though the popular hooks strike a common medium. A size 3, for instance, has a shank of one inch in length, and you should consult the catalogue when ordering hooks to make sure you are sent the correct length of shank. There are two variations to these hooks. The 'Dee' salmon hooks are similar, except that they have a slightly longer shank (one size up). These are intended for certain rivers of fast flow, like the Spey and the Dee. There are also Limerick hooks, which are bronzed and have a down-turned eye. I like to make a salmon fly on a Limerick hook, for the eye is out of the way of the wing roots. The sizes are in the same scale as the 'Ordinary Forged'.

We are now concerned with the special 'Low Water' hooks, for they are of finer wire, though somewhat longer than the standard hooks. I keep these in three sizes, 6, 4, and 8.

Before we study the particular, it is worth glancing at the general effect of the fly. The body is shortened, and does not occupy the full length of the hook-shank. The actual length is left to personal style, but I feel that the shortening is often exaggerated, and I aim at using a little more than half the length, myself. The body must also be slim. The tying silk is gossamer, body silks are kept thin, and dubbings are sparse. The wing sections are meagre, and tied low to the hook.

Tying the Low Water Thunder and Lightning

Let me turn again to a favourite pattern, the Thunder and Lightning, for in this book this fly goes through the metamorphosis, from tube to low water, and, later, to standard strip-wing salmon fly.

The hook is fixed firmly in the vice, the gossamer silk is run on near the eye, and then spiralled down to a point just beyond half-way along the shank. In fact, the silk marks out the limits of the body, a useful practice in all fly dressing.

Fig. 18. Completed tail section of an orthodox salmon fly

At the end of the body, tie in a small length of round gold tinsel, and make three turns round the shank, then tie off. A small length of yellow floss silk butts up against this, making the 'tag' section, which must be kept down to the smallest fraction of an inch. The small golden pheasant crest feather is tied in next, on top of the hook so that it cocks up

71

cheekily. First, however, these crests have to be prepared, both for the tails of salmon flies as well as for the 'topping' which follows the outside curve of the wing.

These 'toppings', as they are called, come from the skull of the golden pheasant. The crests used for the tails are naturally small, and are often sufficiently curved and straight to use direct from the skin. The long ones required for the final 'halo' to the wing are usually flattened and twisted. They have to be straightened and given the correct curve before they can be tied in. The traditional way was by soaking the feather in saliva, and sticking it to the inside of a wineglass; when it was dry, the topping would take on the curve of the glass. My own method of forming the topping is to complete the flies up to that stage, and, keeping the dressings secure with a whip turn or two, remove them from the vice. I strip the shorter fibres away from the roots of the crest feathers, and moisten the toppings thoroughly. Then I lay them out on a flat mirror, and, fitting the fly against its chosen crest, I make the curve to follow the outer curve of the wing. The topping sticks to the smooth glass until it is dry, and maintains the curve that I have given it, while the flatness of the surface takes out any twist.

Now, let us lay aside the topping until we come to making such a wing section. Having tied in the tail, the roots are trimmed away neatly, and the oval tinsel ribbing tied in, following by a length of floss silk. The floss silk body starts cleanly from the tail, but after a turn, an orange hackle is nipped in by the tip. This is done by the floss silk, for the tying thread has been returned to the point from where it started. Now this hackle should be 'doubled'; that is to say

Fig. 19. Appearance of hackle before and after doubling

the fibres are folded against each other in order that they will all slope backwards as the hackle is wound.

As all salmon flies have doubled hackles, we shall pause here to see how this is done. Firstly, I strip away the base fibres, and pull the remaining fibres at right-angles to their stalk, thus separating the point for tying in. Now, attaching a hackle pliers to the base and another to the tip, the hackle lies across the forefinger, the back (dull side) being uppermost. The right-hand fibres can then be stroked to the left by the thumb. If I start from the base, completing a small section at the time, I will manage to double the entire hackle. It helps if the feather is moistened first.

Once doubled, the hackle is tied in to the top of the hook so that the fibres point to the rear when winding. The silk body is completed, and the ribbing is next spiralled up the body, followed by the hackle, which follows its turns. I try to make the hackle stalk lie against the rear of the tinsel as closely as possible. These items are then bound down, and the remnants snipped away.

The throat hackle is from a blue jay. These are the small black and blue barred feathers from a jay's wing, such as countrymen often wear in their hats. Although they are wound in the normal fashion, the stalk of this feather is rather thick. The dull feathers are stripped from one side of the feather, and the stalk is carefully whittled to a manageable thickness with a razor blade. The hackle is tied in by the tip or base, according to the side of the bird it came from. After winding in, the fibres are divided on top of the hook, and pulled down into the normal wet fly position. An alternative method, which I prefer, is simply to tear out a bunch of fibres and tie them below the shank as if they were a bunch of hair. If you find this hard, try turning the hook upside down in the vice.

The wings are tied in next. These are two strips of brown mallard. In all larger flies, it is better to remove these strips from the opposing feathers so that a modicum of quill still attaches to the base. This helps to prevent the fibres from splitting, and makes the slips easy to handle. It also means that the winging slips must be torn from the feather, not cut. If the poor quality fibres at the bottom of the feather are first torn away, you can then work along the quill, marking out each required section with the dubbing needle, before twitching it out smartly.

The two slips must be slim for a low water fly, and remember that if there is an unsightly lump left by the hackle, then the wings will cock up into the air. Hence my own preference for using a bunch of hackle fibres! The wings present no problems that were not overcome in the chapter on wet flies with soft wings. After they have set to your own satisfaction, you must tie in the two small jungle cock cheeks. The soft feathers are plucked off, leaving the two distinct eyes, or one in a small feather. They are secured against the wing, one at a time, with a couple of turns of thread. Then, by pulling the 'eye' through the silk by its stalk, it can be persuaded to lie flat against the wing. When using a jungle cock cheek over a soft feather like mallard, I often varnish the back of the 'eye' to make it stick to the wing, for this keeps it flat and helps the wing to stay together in actual fishing.

No one can pretend that jungle cock is cheap. It may well be outside your price range, and I could not blame you for that. Nor are the hard plastic substitutes of any use at all, but cheer up! Many low water flies do not have them and who can say that this Thunder would not take a salmon with the eyes omitted? Later, I shall discuss how a head can be built up for an eye to be painted on the side, and the Americans have some ingenious transfers which are most effective. Meanwhile, you can try two hackle points from bright yellow cock as a worthwhile substitute.* It works.

In low water salmon flies, as in the other patterns, the general rule of 'left-hand feather for left-hand wing' applies. However, there are exceptions to this, especially if you require the wing to sweep upwards. The Logie has a most pleasing effect caused by two strips of yellow swan sweeping upwards, while they are surmounted by brown mallard, curving downwards. Of course, the swan wings were set the other way round; that is the left-hand feather provided the right-hand wing. Experiment and you will discover what I mean.

Having completed the wing sections, it only remains to tie in the topping which has been prepared as described. The stalk at the base must be gently nicked and bent to form a foot for tying in. Some practice will be needed before the topping will assume its position. I have called it a 'halo' to the wings, and ideally its tip should mate with the tip of the tail crest, thus forming an ellipse, within which lies the wing section. This takes a bit of doing, but meanwhile it is as well to bear in mind that the effect is rather more pleasing to the human eye than impressive to the salmon.

* In recent years the jungle cock has been a protected species, and fly tyers have had to use commercial substitutes.

Materials

Let us now add a few items to our collection so that a selection of low water flies may be dressed.

Low water salmon hooks, sizes 4, 6, 8.
Cock's hackles, yellow, red, blue, green, black, orange, claret.
Jay's hackles.
Round silver and gold tinsel.
Toppings – it is best to buy the whole crest for various sizes.
Jungle cock eyes.

Add to your stock of floss silks; useful colours are black, lemon, blue, usually pale, and red, and white.

Wings – larger sizes of brown mallard, teal, and swan in white, red, blue, yellow and green.

14 How to Make a Strip-Wing Salmon Fly and a Whole Feather-Wing Fly

Now let us turn to the fully-dressed, standard salmon fly. Having worked with small hooks, the huge iron rearing up in the vice appears to be forbidding. Yet, although the materials are larger and more numerous, and even some of the procedures are quite complex, no one who has come with me so far should baulk at the thought of attempting these works of art. Remember from the start, that the tail and final topping form an elliptical 'halo' within which lies the wing section. Remember, too, that the stouter tying silk, 'Naples' is less wasteful than the fine gossamer, and allows you to exert considerably more pressure on the thread. I see little reason why an expedition to the local haberdashery should not yield some synthetic threads in nylon, polythene, or terylene, for I have experimented successfully with these. Indeed, since the colour of the thread is not so vital, it is convenient to work with a light-coloured thread, say of yellow, which shows up well against the black shank of the hook.

Tying a Strip-Wing Salmon Fly

In this group of salmon flies are found such old favourites as the Lady Amherst, the March Brown and the Claret Alder. I prefer to illustrate my methods of tying this fly with the ever-popular Thunder and Lightning, for we have already collected many of the materials, and we can see how the same pattern rings the changes between tube, low water, and now the fully-dressed standard fly.

As in trout flies, the prescription of a salmon fly is listed as briefly as possible, so that the dresser understands which materials to lay out on his bench. At first sight, the range of materials is alarming, but, on reflection, you will realize that one feather or reel of floss will serve for dozens of flies of different patterns.

Here is the formula for the Thunder and Lightning:

Tag – Round gold tinsel and yellow floss.
Tail – Golden pheasant and Indian crow (substitute).
Butt – Black ostrich herl.
Body – Black floss.
Rib – Oval gold tinsel.
Hackle – Hot orange cock.
Throat – Speckled guinea fowl dyed blue.
Wings – Brown mallard.
Sides – Jungle cock.
Topping.

At this stage, it is worth pointing out a few facts. Many dressers will omit the Indian crow tail, and rely simply on the golden pheasant. This apart, I often modernize the fly slightly by using golden lurex as a ribbing, and I introduce fluorescence by substituting D.F.M. wool for the yellow floss tail; in case I have to cope with coloured water, I also use a hackle coloured by a fluorescent dye. These dyes can be readily supplied by the dealer, and are as simple to use as the ordinary ones. As I have pointed out previously, if you cannot run to jungle cock, use two yellow hackle points, which may also be fluorescent.

Having gripped the selected size of hook in the vice, run on the silk, and formed the tag, tail and butt as described before, nip in the tinsel immediately to the right of the ostrich herl, and return the thread to the throat of the hook, where you started. You will have noticed how each new material neatly covers the untidy ends of the previous one. Thus the ostrich herl disguises the roots of the tail and the clipped end of the yellow floss tag. It is hard to find an ostrich herl with a bushy flue, and for this reason, I rarely strip one side of the herl as other dressers do. Four turns of the herl usually make an effective butt.

Two points emerge. It is as important to ensure that the tinsel and silk sections have smooth beds of tying silk to lie on as it was in the trout flies. The place to start making your tail section is largely a matter of taste according to your own notions of the sort of fly you want. The modern tendency is for a slight shortening of the body, but I make my first turn of tinsel for the tag just above the point of the barb, and my whole tail section, from tag to butt, occupied a length of shank equal to the hook-point.

The silk is tied in at the throat and wound to the butt, neatly covering the untidy ends of ostrich herl and ribbing. The ribbing can make an ugly lump if tied in without care.

My own method is to strip away the outer metal covering for a fraction of an inch, exposing the silk core. This can be bound down so that the metal butts up against the hook-shank without being trapped by the thread. Of course, lurex eliminates this. The silk itself should be fanned out between finger and thumb to make a smooth body as it is being wound.

Having reached the tail, the silk makes a turn or two back towards the head, nipping in the doubled orange hackle as described in the previous chapter. The silk continues back to the throat position, and the aim should be to produce a gradual taper from throat to tail. Now, the hackle is wound, following the tinsel ribbing, and tied off. The blue hackle is tied in, and pulled below the hook as described previously.

Two strips of brown mallard are taken from the opposing feathers, and care should be taken to see that a strip of the quill adheres to the fibres. They are positioned so that the topping sheath will form the ellipse of which I have told you. Select the correct position before tightening the thread. If the ends of the wings just meet the tip of the tail, they will be perfect. The standard fly has downswept wings; that is right-hand feather for the right side of the fly. The jungle cock sides are now tied in, one at a time, and you must take care to see that they are matched by looking down on them from above. After a few turns have been made over their stems, a slight pull on the stalks before they are trimmed away will make them lie flat. I always smear a thin coat of varnish on the 'eyes' on the underside, when I want them to lie against mallard or teal, for this helps the fibres of the wings to cling together in use. The topping now completes the fly, save for the varnishing of the head with two coats of 'cellire,' followed, when dry, by black varnish.

Tying a Whole Feather-Wing Fly

The fly we have just dressed is not far removed from the sea trout patterns we made earlier. Now, let us progress one stage farther, to the whole-feather wing patterns. This fly lives up to its name, for the wings are made from whole feathers, usually golden pheasant tippets, outside two narrow strips. Some well-loved names crop up in the lists of patterns, such as the Orange Parson, Black Dose and Sir Herbert, but it is the Durham Ranger that takes my fancy, and illustrates our problems into the bargain.

Once again, I draw up the fly's lineage, so that you will

become accustomed to translating our vocabulary into action. It is listed as follows:

Tag – Round silver tinsel.
Tail – A topping and Indian crow.
Butt – Black ostrich herl.
Body – In four sections, lemon floss, orange, Fiery brown and black seal's fur.
Ribs – Flat silver tinsel and twist.
Hackle – Badger, dyed yellow.
Throat – Light blue.
Wings – A pair of jungle cock, covered by two pairs of tippets. Topping over all.
Sides – Jungle cock.
Cheeks – Blue kingfisher.

Fig. 20. Exploded wing section of the Durham Ranger

In practice, I omit the Indian crow tail and the silver twist. Again, silver lurex would give us all the desired increase of flash.

The tail and body sections will not provide any difficulties that have not been overcome previously. The dubbing of the

79

seal's fur is much thicker than in the trout flies, and it assists greatly if liquid wax is used rather than solid. The seal's fur may also be worked in with a modicum of teased-out wool of similar colour.

The winging procedures are fairly simple. A pair of long jungle cock eye feathers are tied in, back to back, so that their tips extend to the tail. The tippets are positioned, shiny side outwards, so that they veil this centre section over three-quarters of its length. These are easily tied in if the stalks are nicked and prepared in the same way as described for toppings. The jungle cock sides are smaller 'eyes', and tied in the usual fashion, but these too are veiled by the small blue kingfisher feathers, tied in as the 'cheeks'. The soft, base fibres must be stripped, or better still, cut short so that their stiff stubs help to key the feathers in position. The toppings are added, and the fly varnished.

This is the standard tying, but dressers might care to experiment with some of my personal ideas, which are meant to be severely practical rather than picturesque!

Firstly, instead of the centre section being made of jungle cock, I substitute two yellow cock's hackles, and in the smaller patterns, I reduce the two pairs of tippets to a single pair. Again, two 'flashes' of blue cock's hackle points make an effective substitute for the kingfisher cheeks, which, in their turn, are a substitute for the unobtainable blue chatterer feathers.

There are two small groups of salmon flies which are virtually strip-wings, and may be discussed in this chapter, for the fly dressing techniques are very similar to those that I have outlined. These groups are the Dee and Spey flies. These two rivers both have fast currents, and the special qualities of the flies for these conditions are a lightness of dressing, and long flowing hackles. The reader may well consult the book of patterns for the details of materials required, and proceed with confidence.

In the Spey patterns, the tail section is absent, and the body is straightforward, except that there are usually three ribbing materials, one being wound in the opposite way to the other two and hackle. The hackles are invariably long, heron being a popular choice. The main difference lies in the wings, for although they are simple strips, say of brown mallard, they are not pulled down directly to the top of the hook-shank, but rather do they cover the shoulder of hook. This is achieved by tying in one wing at a time, which is held against the side of the shank, towards the top.

Many dressers reverse the direction of the winding of the thread for tying in the further wing, but I have found that with care, this is unnecessary.

These flies are rather uncommon, and since the processes hold no fears for any dresser who has advanced this far, I will content myself by referring him to John Veniard's excellent *Fly-dresser's Guide* for further details of patterns.

15 How to Make Mixed-Wing and Built-Wing Salmon Flies

This is the last stage of fly dressing that we shall encounter, apart from what I might term the 'gimmicks', and which I shall discuss in my last chapter. Between these stages of fly dressing lie many 'in-between' flies which do not occupy a place in the book. More and more of these flies enter the lists each year, as modern anglers grow impatient with traditional techniques, and seek to achieve similar effects more cheaply and with greater ease. For example, I have not mentioned by name that modern killer, the Thurso Copper King, but if you have mastered all the processes discussed in this book, when you find the details of dressing that pattern, you will have no trouble. As I try to make each step follow on from the previous ones in logical sequence, so I nominate a pattern that acts as a bridge, employing many of the materials and techniques of flies dressed previously, yet still introducing new ideas. My bridge between the whole-feather wing flies and those of mixed-wings is a pattern known as the 'Black Dose'.

Mixed-Wing Flies

A mixed wing is simply one made from the fibres of different feathers. If you study a feather with a good magnifying glass, you will find that the fibres are held together by tiny, interlocking hooks. In fact, if you pull a feather to pieces, you should be able to reconstruct it in its original form by lining up the separate fibres and causing these hooks to interlock, or 'marry' in fly dressing language. How is this done?

Holding the fibres in the right order, length, and facing upwards or downwards together, gently stroke them towards their tips and downwards in their natural curve. A little practise will show that this is quite easily achieved, for it is a useful thing to remember when you accidentally split a wing that you are preparing for a trout fly.

Now, if this can be done with fibres from the same feather, so can fibres from different feathers be built up

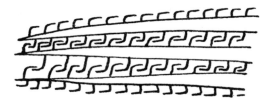

Fig. 21. Wing fibres married together to make composite wing

into a complex wing of different colours, provided that these fibres are taken from the same side of the bird, i.e. all left-hand feathers, for example. Some of these built wings may have fibres from six or seven separate feathers, though as only two or three fibres will be taken from each feather, the drain on stocks is not as severe as might appear at first. The fibres from certain birds marry very easily, such as swan, goose, turkey, and the 'strong' feathers generally. The soft feathers like barred mallard or teal are a little more tricky to manage, and as in other methods of winging, it is best to leave the sections on the quill.

As a rule, the wings made up from right-hand feathers are for the right wing of the fly, and vice versa, though it is as well to note here that large sections of golden pheasant tail tend to fly apart unless they are used on opposite sides. This is more apparent when these feather sections are used as separate wings or under-wings. The beauty of having the 'right to right and left to left' arrangement is that the natural curve of the feathers is suited to the shape of the final topping. Some feathers have a central quill, and the fibres for the mixed-wing can be culled from the appropriate side. Finally, it is a good plan to prepare the wings in advance, and slip them into envelopes marked 'left' and 'right', which can be kept pressed flat under a heavy book until required.

To have an idea of how these mixed wings fit in to a salmon fly, let us examine the materials for the Black Dose.

Tag – Round silver tinsel and light orange floss.
Tail – A topping and married narrow strips of teal and scarlet swan, back to back.

83

Body – A quarter of pale blue seal's fur, the remainder black seal.

Rib – Oval silver.

Hackle – Black cock.

Throat – Light claret.

Wings – A pair of tippets, veiled by married strands of scarlet and green swan, light mottled turkey tail and golden pheasant tail. Peacock herl in strands above.

Again, there are no new problems until the wing sections are reached, and even here, the basis is the same as in the whole feather-wing fly. After the tippets have been tied in to your satisfaction, the outer wings are placed in position on each side of the tippets. This word 'veiling' means that we must not obscure entirely the inside section. Usually the veil covers the middle or upper sections of the wing, and is a trifle shorter. Having positioned them as desired, the thread is tightened, and the wings made secure in the usual way. Any strands of wing that have split can usually be re-united with the main wing by gently stroking along and downwards.

The final topping to this fly is unusual, for it comes from the herl of the sword tail of a peacock. These are the same herls that are used in trout flies such as the Alexandra, and present no problems.

It will be found that some mixed-wings do not easily adopt the natural curve that we love to see on the back of

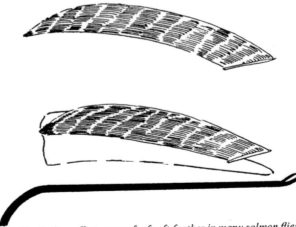

Fig. 22. Veiling effect, on roof, of soft feather in many salmon flies

a salmon fly. Before these wings are tightened on to the hook-shank, they must be 'humped'. This is the same process of stroking towards the tips, and pulling downwards to give the whole wing that half-moon shape. It helps if the wings are moistened slightly, and the process can be done again after the wings have been tied in.

The so-called veiling effect is often achieved in many patterns by using soft feathers such as teal, mallard and summer duck. These feathers are often married together in strips, as described. Sometimes it is worthwhile to stick them to the inner wings with clear varnish before they are tied in. The entire wing section then can be put on at once. Of course, the varnish should be allowed to dry first, and, if possible, the adhesive parts of the wing should be to the right of the thread, so that they can be removed with the spare roots.

I am not going to pretend that these wings are easy to prepare and tie on, but practise will bring perfect results in time. Start off with those flies that employ fewer married sections, such as some of the low water patterns or the Tom Tickler, which only has two, or else dress some of your own sea trout and lake flies with simple mixed wings of two sections. Some patterns like the Reckless William, lend themselves to this treatment.

Finally, the salmon will not know if one fibre is out of place, for the flowing current will disturb them in any case. These flies are really art-forms in their own right, and you may find excellent ways of showing them off, in paper weights, picture frames, brooches for example. Yet many great names stand out from the lists, such as the Silver Grey, the Black Doctor, Green Highlander and many others.

Built-Wing Flies

The pinnacle of the fly dresser's art is the construction of the built-wing fly, for the wings are constructed of some sections, usually three in number, that must overlap each other like the scales of a fish. The final section is often of mallard, and it forms the 'roof' of the fly. The second section is usually a pair of mixed wings, and they fit over a pair of inner wings, such as a pair of tippets, or strips of white-tipped turkey tail, tied in back to back.

I will describe how I dress one of these flies, the well-known Dusty Miller. Firstly, let us study its pedigree:

Tag – Silver tinsel (round) and yellow floss.
Tail – A topping and Indian crow.
Butt – Black ostrich.
Body – two-thirds silver tinsel (embossed) remainder orange floss.
Rib – Fine oval silver tinsel.
Hackle – Golden olive cock over orange floss only.
Throat – Speckled guinea fowl (gallina).
Wings – A pair of black, white-tipped strips of turkey tail back to back. Overlapping these, a mixed sheath of married strands of teal, yellow, scarlet and orange swan, bustard, florican, and golden pheasant tail; married narrow strips of pintail, summer duck, and narrow strips of brown mallard over.
Cheeks – Jungle cock.

Once again, our immediate problem lies in the wings, for the body, hackles and tail sections are quite straightforward. The underwing is prepared first, being two narrow strips cut from the dark turkey tail, with well-marked white tips. The strips should be quite narrow, and put together back to back in the left to left, right to right position. When tied in, they should lie low to the body.

The first 'married' wings are tied in next, but the feather slips from the left-hand feathers take up the right-hand wing. Care should be taken to see that the tips and base of the turkey strips are exposed. The second 'married' sections go on next, that is the strips of pintail and summer duck, again 'left to left'. Finally, the roof is put on as described in the section on wings of brown mallard. These strips should overlap the mixed wings but not completely. The jungle cock cheeks are tied in, and the head varnished.

Although every one of these processes has been discussed, considerable care will be needed in the positioning of the wing sections. Personally I prefer to use feather strips of narrow proportions and to take time with the fly.

There is one other process that has to be mentioned in this section, and that is the veiling of the bodies of some patterns with the small toucan feathers. This is not done in the Dusty Miller, but other flies, such as the Jock Scott, do make use of it.

These flies have their bodies divided into sections, but there is a further butt of herl between them. Just below this butt, the hook is veiled with toucan. These feathers are very fragile, but there is no difficulty in tying them in. The fluffy base fibres are stripped away, leaving the central stalk. They are quite small, and two, three or more will have to be placed on top of each other. They are then tied down to the hook-shank, one bunch on top, the other immediately below, to achieve the delicate veiling effect around the body material. The ostrich herl butt neatly covers the roots and bindings.

Materials for Salmon Flies

The collecting of materials for the salmon flies dressed in these last chapters does pose some questions. The hooks will be bought in your favourite sizes, and if you do have trouble with the upturned eye, there is no reason why you should not use the bronze Limerick patterns, though in my opinion, they do not please the eye so much. The body materials, such as flosses, seal's fur can be obtained, but an entire range would naturally be expensive. On the other hand, you may supplement your supply by cadging wool from the needlewoman of the house, for indeed many new patterns are based on the 'Berlin' wools, though others are equally as good.

Hackles are not too difficult to obtain in the sizes required for salmon flies. Roughly speaking, these vary in length from 2-inch hackles for the smallest flies to 6 inches for the largest flies ever made, but such as which are very rare nowadays. Around 4 inches is a fine average length, for you may always trim a hackle, but never add to it. The colours are in the main similar to those discussed in other chapters, but you may still dye those delicate shades, or buy them. Guinea fowl, natural and blue is used extensively, as is cock.

Tails and toppings are the golden pheasant feathers I have mentioned, best bought in quantity on the skin if you intend to tie many flies. Salmon patterns run away with them. Normally, it is quite safe to omit additional tail feathers, like Indian crow, but the substitute, which I think is equally as good, is quite inexpensive. Herls for butts should also be bought or purloined from Victorian hats. The standby is ostrich dyed black, but again, wool will serve at a pinch, especially while practising.

It is the wings that cause us to run an overdraft. But consider how many of them come from the Christmas turkey. The cinnamon tail feathers are excellent substitutes for the peacock's wing, while the brown mottled tail feather does service for the rare bustard. From the turkey, we also obtain the white-tipped feather we have just used in the

Dusty Miller, and as the larger flies use these strips in double sections, they do not last long. Light speckled turkey, oak turkey, and grey mottled turkey all find a niche in the salmon fly dresser's heart. The moral is to buy your bird, direct from the farmer, and to pluck it yourself.

Dyed swan and goose is used to make our mixed wings. They are quite cheap, and last for many dozens of patterns. Golden pheasant tails, and those from the guinea fowl seem to be plentiful at present, but there is no denying that other feathers are either very costly or impossible to find. I have not been able to buy any pintail for some time, and even the other barred feathers, mallard, teal, widgeon, are scarce at times, while summer duck is like gold-dust.

The answer is to improvise, and I shall discuss the implications of this in the next chapter. It is now common practice to leave out certain sections of mixed-wing flies, and the remaining strips are simply larger. As for the married sections of mallard and summer duck, you must either leave out the latter, or content yourself with another material, such as teal. The same applies to pintail. I could go on, for at one time, many patterns had horns of macaw, but where are they now? And of the price of jungle cock, the least said the better. My advice on these materials, is to collect what you can find and afford; for the rest, use your imagination for substitutes or omissions. The salmon will never know.

16 Modern Trends in Fly Tying

You will have noticed that I have described the traditional processes of fly tying, without describing in detail the use of modern plastics and the like. It is very true that if you master the processes, then the patterns will look after themselves. If you can tie a Peter Ross, the simple Polystickle has no terrors. Due to the pace of modern life, the demand for instant success, even in fly fishing, there's little patience today for ancient, painstaking craftsmen. I hope you will join the minority of fly tyers who make a fly, not just for its practical application, but because 'a thing of beauty is a joy for ever . . .'

It would be hard for me to keep pace with the invention of new patterns. Every fishing journal I open contains at least one miracle fly. The trouble is that most of these will be forgotten, not having stood the one supreme test, the test of time. Often the inventor of a new pattern, while proclaiming the qualities of his own wonder will seek to enhance its glory by denigrating traditional patterns. History proves that Invictas and Peter Ross will be killing trout long after his wonder fly is forgotten. While welcoming the new imitative flies, especially on still water, plus a handful of other patterns which prove their success, it would be mere folly to discount those standard patterns which have served us so well for so long.

The Muddler Effect

The Muddler Minnow is new to us. It is not a new pattern. It's an American importation, invented by Don Gapen many years ago as a copy of a local small fish called the Cockatush Minnow. Although it was intended for bass, it soon became ubiquitous as a killer of trout and salmon, or indeed of any predator of small fish. The standard pattern is brown, but coloured variations – orange, yellow, black and white – are common on both sides of the 'Big Drink'.

The only tying process which is new in the Muddler is making the collar of deer's hair at the throat. It is quite simple, once it is remembered that the hair will only spin

89

round a bare hook-shank, so there must be no underlay of tying thread. A small bunch of the hair is laid on top of the shank, a loop of tying silk put over it, which, when pulled tight, has the dual effect of spinning the hair round the shank, and making it stand out at right angles to it. The next bunch is tied in close in front, and so on until the head is finished, when the hair is trimmed short to the desired amount. I find it best to tie in the hair with the tips to the rear of the hook.

This closely cropped deer-hair may be added to a whole range of flies. Any lure can be 'muddlified', the Whiskey Muddler being but one example. Unsinkable sedges can have their bodies made in this way. A small, short ruff may convert any nymph into its hatching version, as in the Olive, Sedge or Buzzer versions for example.

Another plastic much in use is sheet polythene, as in the Polystickle series. Transparency has long been used in fly tying, as in Dunne's series of dry fly, using oiled rayon floss, or Newskin (Collodian) for the Copper Boy, an effective Buzzer Pupa imitation. The medium grade of polythene is best, cut into thin strips, and stretched before winding. More transparent effects can be obtained by building up coats of varnish, or liquid plastic (Vycoat).

Bucktails and streamers are now being applied widely on reservoirs. Although the impression may be given that these are new, they, too, are mostly importations from the U.S.A. sometimes with slight variations. A black body and hair-wing, sometimes with a coloured aiming point to prevent short takes, is very popular, as in the long-standing American Black Gordon and its near relative, the Sweeney Todd. Such flies involve no new fly-tying processes, and the wing can be made from buck-tail, squirrel, or even goat-hair according to budget or taste.

Streamer flies involve wings of four long cock-hackles tied together on top of the hook. Many interesting colour effects can be had by laying one shade of hackle on top of the other. The tying process is simply to strip the bottom of the stalks, match the hackles, then tie them on as the normal wing of a wet fly. American literature is rich in patterns, some of which find their way here, others yet to come, while the field of experimentation is wide, to get perchy or roachy effects. The sinuous working of the wing is its killing factor.

Bloggs's Green Nymph!

One modern trend is confusing. This is the change from the fly bearing its inventor's name to that of the tyer. Today there can be nothing new in the making of nymphs with hair or herl. Skues, Kite and Sawyer explored this field thoroughly enough. Yet, Bloggs will produce a Green Nymph, or what-have-you, from dyed herl the only original part of which is the name! We have also to contend with tyers who change a standard pattern slightly, giving it their name. Invictas with green or brown bodies appear, but Ogden, not Bloggs, invented the killing Invicta, and if it kills with a green body as well as a yellow, Ogden rather than Bloggs should be coming across.

Who Ties Flies Now?

When this book first appeared my fly-tying classes were an oasis in a desert, especially in southern England. The scene has changed out of all recognition. There are numerous evening classes in most parts of the country. A fly-tyers guild has also been formed with members both at home and abroad, and it publishes a monthly newsletter covering developments and techniques of fly tying. At the time of writing, its secretary is J. Denford, 7 Colley Close, Worthy Road, Winchester, Hants. Every keen fly tyer should belong to the guild.

One remaining question is to what extent the 'amateur fly' will replace the professional product. The sad truth is that the British 'pro' is a dying breed. The big tackle houses have closed their fly-tying rooms. For reasons of cost and organization it is hard to run fly tying on an 'outworker' basis. Our 'cheap fly' tradition has destroyed much of our craftsman-tied flies, and I know skilled lady tyers who have turned to 'charring' to eke out the family budget. Those ladies, trained expertly before the war, have few successors. At last Britain is importing flies from the low labour-cost areas of the world, Africa, Hong Kong and Japan. True, some fly-tying firms survive here, as do individual 'pros', but I feel that the future lies with home-tied flies.

This will change the whole atmosphere of fly tying, so that it becomes as integral a part of our sport as casting itself. Nor should it be viewed in isolation, for many a student of my classes has asked me at the start of a course, 'do you only do fly tying?' only to confess at its end how it had opened up a full understanding of our sport. It relates the separate entities of fly fishing, the casting to the retrieve, the entomology to the feeding behaviour of the trout. In short, it turns the fly fisherman into the complete man.

Let me end by driving home the final message, that there's no such thing as a fly pattern. There are only fly-tying processes. You don't learn to tie a Peter Ross or a Muddler Minnow. You only learn how to work with silk, fur and feather. The aim is not to be able to tie that Peter Ross. The aim is to be able to understand our way of writing out fly 'prescriptions', so that on the bench you can turn out any pattern from the simple nymph, winged dry fly, right through to the married-wing salmon fly. This is what any fly-tying course should achieve, be it book or class. And unless the teacher is firstly competent in these processes, then in this diploma-free art, his pupils would also fall short of all-round ability. Our first attempts catch fish. Our final aim is only perfection!

Book List

The author recommends the following authorities for details of the dressing of artificial flies:

Geoffrey Bucknall, *Fly-fishing Tactics on Still Water*, Frederick Muller.

A. Courtney Williams, *A Dictionary of Trout Flies*, A. & C. Black.

John Goddard, *The Super Flies of Still Water*, Ernest Benn.

John Goddard, *Trout Flies of Still Water*, A. & C. Black.

J. R. Harris, *An Angler's Entomology*, Collins.

T. C. Ivens, *Still Water Fly Fishing*, André Deutsch.

T. Donald Overfield, *Fifty Favourite Nymphs*, Ernest Benn.

Tom Stewart, *Two Hundred Popular Flies and how to tie them*, Ernest Benn.

John Veniard, *Fly-dresser's Guide*, A. & C. Black.

John Veniard, *A Further Guide to Fly-dressing*, A. & C. Black.

C. F. Walker, *Lake Flies and Their Imitation*, Herbert Jenkins.

Richard Walker, *Fly Dressing Innovations*, Ernest Benn.

Index

Advanced wing style 34–35

Beetles 55–56
Bench for fly tying 7
Black and Peacock Spider 10–14
Black Dose 83–85
Black Spider 16
Blue Dun 31–32
Bobbin-holder 7
Built-wing flies 85–87

Cholmondeley-Pennell (hook) scale 11
Cinnamon Sedge 36–38
Corixa 55–56

D.F.M. (daylight fluorescent materials) 43
Down-eyed hook 11
D.R.F. (depth ray fire) wool 43
Dry fly 3
    fine wire hooks 11
    hackled 18–23
    rolled-wing 36–38
    split-wing 31–35
Dubbing needle 5–7
Durham Ranger 78–80
Dusty Miller 85–87
Dyeing materials 58–60

Entomology 2

Fanwings 48–50
Fluorescence detector 8

Ginger Quill 21–23
'Gossamer' tying thread 11
Greenwell's Glory 21, 24–29

Hackle guard 19
Hackle pliers 5
Hackles 18–21, 34
    colours 20–21
    doubled 72, 73
    winding on 12–14, 18–20
Hair for fly dressing 57–61
Halford, F. M., doctrine of imitation 2–3
Herl 11, 12
Hooks 8, 11
    for salmon flies 70–71
    scales of sizes 11
    testing 11

Imitation of food-forms 2, 3

Landrail 37
Lighting 7
Low water salmon flies 70–75
Lurex 43

Magnifying glasses 7–8
Mallard and Claret 40–41
Mallard feathers 39
Materials 16–17, 23, 29–30, 38, 43, 44, 46, 51, 56, 60, 69, 75, 87–88
Mayfly, and life cycle 45–46
Mayfly (artificial) 46–51
    plastic bodies 50
Mixed-wing flies 82–85
Muddler Minnow 89–90

'Naples' silk 42
Nylon tying thread 43
Nymphs 53, 54–55

Peacock herl 11, 12
Peter Ross 41–44

References in bold type are where tying techniques are used for specific patterns.

Pheasant Tail Nymph 54–55
Polythene sheet 90
Primary feathers 26

Razor blades 5
Redditch (hook) scale 11
Rolled-wing dry flies 36–38

Scissors 5
Seal's fur 29
Secondary feathers 26
Silver Blue 66
Silver Doctor 67–68
Spider patterns 16
Split-wing dry flies 31–35
Stoat Tail 64–65
Storage of materials 8
Strip-wing salmon flies 76–78

Teal feathers 39
Thunder and Lightning 67
    low water version 71–74
    strip-wing version 76–78
Tinsel 42

Tube flies 62–69
    types of tubes 62–63
Tying, basic sequence 12
Tying thread 11, 43

Underbody 16

Variants 34
Vice 4–5

Water-boatman 55
Waxing the silk 12, 32
Weighted patterns 16, 54
Wet fly 3
    basic tying 10–14
    hackles 11, 12–14
    soft-winged 39–44
    winged 24–30
Whip finish 7, 14–15
    tool 7
Whole feather-wing flies
    78–80
Winging 24, 25–28, 73–74,
    hair wing 57, 64–65
Winging pliers 7